W9-BXA-699

praise for
PURSUED

"If you've ever read Francine River's book *Redeeming Love,* you must get this book! Jud's PURSUED message brings the story of Hosea and Gomer to life in a way that resonated deep within my heart. As a woman who longs to be accepted despite my faults and shortcomings, this page-turning book was a pure gift of grace and truth. It reads as well as your favorite fiction book but leaves behind life-changing lessons of what it means to be personally loved and adored by God."

—*Lysa TerKeurst, president of Proverbs 31 Ministries, author of* Made to Crave

"My good friend Jud Wilhite has done it again! PURSUED is a fantastic book about God's relentless pursuit of our prodigal race."

—*Andy Stanley, senior pastor of North Point Ministries, author of* The Grace of God

"PURSUED is filled with real-life stories of God-pursued people from Israel to Las Vegas. It will show you God's heart in a way that will change yours."

—*John Ortberg, senior pastor of Menlo Park Presbyterian Church, author of* Who Is This Man?

"You are loved. You are loved. You are loved. This heartbeat of God echoes through eternity. Jud Wilhite combines both beautiful language and compelling stories to remind us of this timeless truth. Wherever you are. Whoever you are. Pick up this book. Read it. You won't be the same."

—*Margaret Feinberg, author of* Wonderstruck *and* Scouting the Divine

"PURSUED is an incredible book that clearly moves the focus from our pursuit of God to God's pursuit of us. Jud sheds light on an often-overlooked part of the Bible and reveals depths of God's grace that will breathe new life and energy into you!"

—*Christine Caine, founder of the A21 Campaign, author of* Undaunted

"Does it seem odd to talk about God's obsession with you? It won't after reading PURSUED; it may actually seem like an understatement. This remarkable book will challenge how you see God and faith and help you experience God at deeper levels of your life."

—*Mark Batterson, lead pastor of National Community Church, author of* The Circle Maker

"Jud Wilhite serves God with a passion to reach broken people for Christ. Through his rich experience as a pastor he has written this book to help all of us discover just how much we are PURSUED by our gracious God. Let go of the things that are holding you hostage and embrace a new level of freedom in Christ."

—*Steven Furtick, lead pastor of Elevation Church, author of* Sun Stand Still

"If you've ever felt like you're too far gone for the love of God, PURSUED is for you. Jud Wilhite masterfully combines biblical truths with real-life examples to reveal the never-ending, loving pursuit of God."

—*Craig Groeschel, senior pastor of LifeChurch.tv, author of* Soul Detox: Clean Living in a Contaminated World

"I just finished reading PURSUED. It changed my life! This book helped me understand that God's correction is for my protection. This book showed me how much God *adores* us! I *really* needed this book in this season of my life. Thanks, Jud Wilhite!"

—*Rev. Run, author of* Words of Wisdom, *founding member of Run-D.M.C., member of the Rock and Roll Hall of Fame*

"This is hands down the most important book you'll read this year. Jud brilliantly helps all of us understand the simple truth that there is a God who is pursuing us with a scandalous love. Whether you're starting a journey with God or you've been a Christ follower for decades, this book can change the way you view God and what he's doing in your life. I'll pick this book up again and again."

—*Pete Wilson, pastor of Cross Point Church,*
author of Plan B *and* Empty Promises

"All too often I hear people say, 'My life was falling apart and then I FOUND GOD!' This statement always causes me to scratch my head, because I was never aware that God was actually the one lost…I was…and He found me! I love this fresh perspective offered to us by Jud in this new book. It's not that we are obsessed with God and are pursuing Him, but rather that He loves us and wants nothing more than to have an active, vibrant, and ongoing relationship with us. You have got to read this book!"

—*Perry Noble, senior pastor of NewSpring Church,*
author of Unleash!

"PURSUED is such a powerful reminder of the greatness of God's love and the persistence of His will for us. This book will open your eyes and renew your faith. For anyone who needs a reminder of the grace of God and the potential of their future, I would highly recommend PURSUED."

—*Matthew Barnett, co-founder of The Dream Center,*
author of The Cause Within You

pursued

God's Divine Obsession with You

JUD WILHITE

New York Boston Nashville

All Scripture quotations, unless otherwise indicated, are taken from the Holy Bible, New Living Translation, copyright © 1996, 2004. Used by permission of Tyndale House Publishers Inc., Carol Stream, Illinois 60188. All rights reserved.

Scripture quotations marked (ESV) are taken from The Holy Bible, English Standard Version, copyright © 2001 by Crossway Bibles, a division of Good News Publishers. Used by permission.

Scripture quotations marked (MSG) are taken from The Message by Eugene H. Peterson. Copyright © 1993, 1994, 1995, 1996, 2000, 2001, 2002. Used by permission of NavPress Publishing Group.

Scripture quotations marked (NIV) are taken from the Holy Bible, New International Version. Copyright © 1973, 1973, 1984, by Biblica, Inc. Used by permission of Zondervan.

FaithWords
Hachette Book Group
237 Park Avenue
New York, NY 10017

www.faithwords.com

Printed in the United States of America

RRD-C

First trade edition: November 2013
10 9 8 7 6 5 4 3 2 1

FaithWords is a division of Hachette Book Group, Inc.
The FaithWords name and logo are trademarks of Hachette Book Group, Inc.

The Hachette Speakers Bureau provides a wide range of authors for speaking events. To find out more, go to www.hachettespeakersbureau.com or call (866) 376-6591.

The publisher is not responsible for websites (or their content) that are not owned by the publisher.

The Library of Congress has cataloged the hardcover edition as follows:

Wilhite, Jud
  Pursued : God's divine obsession with you / Jud Wilhite.
    p. cm.
  ISBN 978-1-4555-1546-2
  1. God--Love. 2. Grace (Theology) 3. Spirituality. 4. Bible. O.T. Hosea--Criticism, interpretation, etc. I. Title.
  BT140.W54 2013
  231'.6--dc23 2012014289

ISBN 978-1-4555-1544-8 (pbk.)

To the One who pursues

Contents

Introduction. Catch Me If You Can 1

Part One. Pursued for Relationship 11

One. The Proposal 13

Two. Passionate Pursuit 31

Three. An Affair to Remember 51

Part Two. Pursued in Grace 71

Four. Bad Romance 73

Five. Loved from Death to Life 88

Six. Price for a Prostitute 105

Seven. Award-Winning Performance 118

Part Three. Pursued to Become 137

Eight. Renewing the Relationship 139

Nine. Living with a New Identity 156

Ten. The Time-Out Chair 169

Eleven. Saint Maybes 184

Conclusion: The Joy of Being Caught 202

Acknowledgments 208

Notes 210

About the Author 214

catch me if you can

I was born the running kind.

—*Johnny Cash*

the first time I stole a car, I was fourteen.

It was 2 a.m. on an arid Saturday morning in March, and some school friends were staying over at my house in Amarillo, Texas. A little bored, we got the not-so-bright idea to sneak out and explore the neighborhood. As we surveyed the block for potential sources of excitement, we discovered that one of my neighbors had left his old brown 1978 Chevy Impala unlocked in his driveway with the keys in the ignition. Jackpot! This was way too much temptation for a pack of adolescent boys.

We pushed the four-door Impala out of the driveway and down the street so no one would hear us start it. Then I jumped behind the wheel (after all, it was my neighborhood so I should get to drive first), gunned the accelerator, and we were on our way. We thought we'd just cruise around town and then bring it back. No one's the wiser, right? No harm, no foul.

We had a blast for the first few minutes. The manual windows were rolled down and the Rolling Stones' "Satisfaction" was cranked up! Then one of my buddies, already a little queasy, got carsick and left some major evidence of our little excursion all over the tan vinyl in the backseat. I knew we couldn't return my neighbor's car with yuck all over it so we found a car wash that was open twenty-four hours and prepared to clean up the mess.

One of the things I love about car washes is the way those industrial-strength vacuum cleaners will suck up everything. Problem solved. It only required four quarters, but after pooling everyone's pocket change, we didn't have it. Fortunately (or so we thought), there was a 7-Eleven convenience store across the street. Since this was his mess, the guy who had thrown up got to go get change while the rest of us waited at the car wash.

As my friend walked out of the convenience store, a black-and-white Amarillo Police car pulled up, complete with the swirling lights on top. No need to panic, I thought. We were parked out of sight of the store, my friend was a pretty good talker, and he'd make up something to tell the officer and be on his way. But to our amazement, the cop put my buddy in the patrol car and drove off.

Here we were, a half hour away from my house—and the owner of the car's house. As soon as the police notified my friend's parents, they would call my parents, since he was spending the night at my house. And we sat in a borrowed car—not stolen, right?—that my neighbor thought was in his driveway. *What were we thinking?*

I drove as fast as I could (not the smartest thing to do, I realize in hindsight), hoping to get home before my dad was awakened by the dreaded phone call. My body literally broke out in a cold sweat. The car interior still smelled rank, and my buddies were frightened and already trying to lay the blame on me. Imagining other cops in pursuit of us, I kept looking over my shoulder. I expected to see blue-and-red lights flashing in the rearview mirror at any moment.

When we pulled up to my house, my dad was standing with his arms crossed at the front door in his light blue cotton robe, house shoes, and white tube socks. He glared at me from below his slightly gray eyebrows before I even got out of the car. At 6-foot-3 and 190 pounds with a full head of salt-and-pepper bed hair sticking up, this former master sergeant in the Army was an imposing figure. I had a lot of explaining to do, and it wasn't going to be easy. Bottom line, we screwed up. Later we found out that the police were looking for a mugger that fit my friend's description perfectly, which was why they immediately picked him up. Needless to say, joyriding didn't hold the same appeal as it once had.

RUNNING ON EMPTY

For years after my carjacking incident, I had recurrent dreams in which I was driving as fast as I could to get away from…the cops…or someone who was after me and going to let me have it once they caught me. It was one of those dreams that usually seemed to coincide with stressful periods in my life, times when I felt anxious and worried about the decisions I was making or the direction I was taking. There were waking moments when I had the same feeling of dread in my gut, the same nervous sensation I was running from something…or someone.

And looking back now, I was definitely running away from the hard realities of life. By the age of seventeen, I was lost in the fog of drug addiction, searching for the next party and another fix, working hard to detach from the pain inside me. Occasionally I'd sober up, once again feeling like a runaway, overwhelmed with the sense someone was after me.

I knew that someone was probably God, chasing after me to write a massive speeding ticket for all the stuff I was doing. He was the ultimate cop waiting to nab me for my crimes, and I was definitely guilty. I'm not sure where I developed this sense of God. Maybe it was my guilty conscience or simply a cultural stereotype I'd picked up. Either way, I just tried to steer clear of all the God questions. I had habits that I didn't want to address. Junk I didn't want to deal with. And a lifetime of crimes and misdemeanors that I didn't want to face.

I ran as hard and as fast as I could for four long years, but eventually I just wore out. I felt so tired. So alone. One night in my bedroom, I got on my knees and quietly gave up. I turned myself in to God and asked for His help.

So much of what is good in my life started there. I learned I was known by God and loved by Him, not because of the good or bad things I had done, but because of *His* goodness. He was no longer the angry, cosmic cop chasing me down. Nor was He the out-of-touch and old-fashioned God reflected in the stained glass windows and upholstered pews of the church my family attended. Of course He is ancient and immense, but I discovered God to be significant, relevant, and involved in every way of my life.

I realized something I've been unraveling ever since—God wasn't pursuing me to give me a ticket and send me to jail. He was pursuing me to give me the life I was meant to live, a life that would display His love and grace for everyone to see. He was serious about wanting to be in a relationship with me. With *me*—the addict, the carjacker, the druggie, the slacker.

What started off so beautiful, freeing, and wonderful, however, soon became tainted with my Christian work ethic. Over the next several years I became the very kind of Christian I had detested—uptight and judgmental. I started substituting my grace-oriented connection with God for a set of suffocating rules and regulations. I worked hard to *continue* to be loved by God, rather than serving *because* God loved me. I performed acts of kindness in order to get things from God rather than doing them simply to enjoy Him.

The Bible became more about what not to do and less about knowing God. I was more concerned about being the moral police to others, rather than compassionately seeking to understand where people were coming from. I worshiped and went to church because God demanded it, not out of gratitude for God's love.

In short, I went through a lengthy season where I became everything I despised about religion—I traded the grace of God for a ball-and-chain life of religious hoop jumping (and it's hard to jump through hoops when you're dragging that kind of hardware around!). I kept running even though I didn't have to. And the most remarkable thing is God's pursuit of me did not stop when I initially surrendered to Him.

Maybe you know what it feels like to be running away from something or someone, always looking over your shoulder and wondering when you'll be caught. You know what it means to feel tired because you can't live up. You go to church, but not enough; pray, but not enough; strive to do right, but not enough. Some days it feels like everything in your faith falls short. You find yourself praying primarily when you are in need or trouble. Reading your Bible is something you think you should do, but there's never enough time to focus and really dig in the way you want. Secretly you find that much of the Bible leaves you confused. Church attendance feels hit or miss, and when you're there, you feel guilty. All of this leads to a cycle of frustration that becomes an obstacle more than an aid. With time commitments and the pressures of life, you aren't really sure where you are spiritually… or where God is anymore.

Frustration and even apathy can grow toward God. You believe the good news of Jesus is good, but it *feels* more like *exhausting* news. Faith has become one more area of life filled with obligation and responsibility. You go through the motions, but it's draining. In those rare quiet moments you have a hunch there must be *more*. Maybe everybody else gets it, but you're not sure you do. You're worn out and stressed out. You've given it your best effort, but you're not convinced it's working.

We're often still running long after we've returned home to God spiritually. We run from our past failures by trying to overcompensate and demonstrate our usefulness to God. We run from the wild grace He offers by trying to advance ourselves in our own strength. We run from the freedom He provides by imprisoning our hearts through chasing after undeserving things. We run from the rest He gives by working harder and harder to measure up when God has said all along that He is enough.

The good news is you don't have to keep running. You don't have to feel alone. There is another way beyond the frustration, fatigue, and even indifference. God is still pursuing you *after* you've placed your faith in Him—not to burden you with more tasks on the to-do list or to whip you into shape, but to love you. He pursues you with an intensity that can breathe life into you.

Pursued is for everyone who is sick and tired of being sick and tired. For everyone buried under the burden of trying to keep it together, for those wrestling with shame, for those who are over faking it, who feel like posers, who know they aren't measuring up and know if people knew half their real story, they'd run out of the room. It's for those who long to know God, but feel something's missing.

In the pages to come, I'd like to explore a kind of intensely personal journey with God. By surveying the unfamiliar *Sin*-derella story of the prophet Hosea and his wife, the prostitute Gomer, a portrait of God's unyielding pursuit and obsessive love emerges that will shock and surprise you. My goal is to help you:

- Discover how a life-giving relationship with God can bring new joy into your life when you're weary and frustrated.
- Move God's grace from your head into deeper places of your heart to stop the exhausting cycles of guilt, shame, and performance before God.
- Find fulfillment for the longing to be pursued by experiencing a perfect love that breaks our unrealistic expectations of others.
- Live passionately with a restored sense of security so you can face relationships and decisions with more confidence.

Returning to the relationship God invites us into empowers us to live fully and completely in His grace.

PROSTITUTES, PROPHETS, AND YOU

When God wanted to illustrate the passion, love, and relationship He desires to have with us, He didn't showcase a lawyer
with a bureaucratic list of "dos and don'ts." He didn't platform
a politician who would introduce strategies to change the world.
He didn't choose a sword-wielding warrior, a power-hungry
monarch, or an invincible superhero. He didn't even choose a
saint or a priest.

He chose a *prostitute* to flip our preconceived ideas about God
and faith upside down.

The story of a prostitute who marries a prophet and the drama
(not to mention the passion, pain, and turmoil) of their relationship in the Biblical book of Hosea still speaks to us today.
The time and place may have changed, but the human heart
and God's love remain the same. In fact, the first time the marriage metaphor is fully explored in the Bible to demonstrate
God's journey with us occurs in the story of the prophet Hosea.
His marriage to Gomer, a practicing prostitute, vividly renders
a flesh-and-blood parable of God's association with His people.
From Hosea forward, the Bible uses marriage as the standard way
of describing the love God longs to show us.

Hosea is so rich with stunning insights into God's passion that
many people don't know what to do with it. When was the last
time you heard a message in church about Hosea? It is a profound book that's been buried under the layers of contemporary
faith. The book is unconventional, but that's precisely part of
why we need to be challenged by it today. Digging up its depths
is like finding treasure that infuses us with renewed perspective.
Taken as a whole, it presents a magnificent mosaic of who God is

for us. It has been right there all along—if we'd just take time to look.

The story of Hosea has moved me past mere business-as-usual stuff with God to gratitude. It jarred me back into wonder at God's mercy when I was just going through the motions. When I felt worn out running after God, Hosea stopped me in my tracks with the incredible realization that God was pursing me! It rattled me out of my indifference and fatigue and led me back into the calm waters of faith, rest, trust, peace, and joy with God.

Hosea's example also shows us that reducing our involvement with God to a lengthy list of obligations not only robs us of the fullness of God's love, but deprives Him of real affectionate participation with us. Instead, God's desire to enjoy communion with us beats at the heart of His eternal story. From the beginning of the Bible when God walked in the Garden, to the end when God comes to dwell with His people forever, the message is not primarily about our pursuit of God, but His pursuit of us. God seeks fellowship with us and persistently overcomes obstacles to that intimacy—namely our sin. His grace is radical, undomesticated, untamed, and unpredictable. His love is as fierce as it is jealous.

It's time to quit running. It's time to quit working hard for something that can't be earned. It's time to expand your view of God and His radical grace and to experience Him more fully and completely. Together we'll see how we can be liberated to discover our true life. To experience the obsessive love of a God who's so much more than we ever imagined.

A God who shockingly pursues us the way a devoted husband pursues the wife he adores.

PART ONE

———————————→

pursued for relationship

CHAPTER ONE

---------->

the proposal

I suppose you could say I'm a quite religious
woman that is very confused about religion.

—Lady Gaga

i'll never forget that sweltering hot 100-degree Texas day—
the kind of heat that leaves you perspiring after a trip to the
mailbox and seems to make the hours pass more slowly. I had
planned out the whole evening and couldn't contain my nervous
excitement as I approached the most important date of my life.
Finally, as six o'clock came, I pulled into Lori's driveway in my
hideous teal green Honda Civic, took a deep breath, and made
my way to the door. As a beginning pastor, I sported my best
brown checkered suit jacket, which wasn't saying much. She answered the door in a stunning black dress. With her dark hair
and gorgeous blue-gray eyes, I felt very much out of my league. I
tried to act normal, making small talk about what we'd done that
day as we headed out for what she thought was a very nice, but
normal date. My plan was to take her for a romantic dinner at the

most elegant restaurant in town and then drive to a nearby park, where I would ask her to marry me.

So far, everything was going perfectly. We arrived at the restaurant, which was on the top floor of the tallest building in our city, and were seated at a table with an incredible view. Only what I saw outside made my stomach tighten. Dark gray storm clouds were rolling in all around us, making it no surprise when I looked out the window a few minutes later and saw it raining—not the gentle, romantic *Singin'-in-the-Rain* kind of rain, but angry, fierce sheets of water that would be at home in *The Perfect Storm*.

I swallowed hard. My carefully orchestrated plan to ask her to marry me at the park washed away before my eyes. I began to panic.

Remaining calm and cool on the outside, I desperately improvised plan B on the spot. I had no choice but to ask her to marry me in the restaurant. Only one problem: the ring was in my car parked outside many stories below us. No big deal, right?

I casually excused myself for the restroom and took the elevator to the bottom floor. After making the mad dash to the car for the ring, I was completely soaked.

"Where have you been?" she asked as I sat back down at the table, acting as if it were totally normal to be drenched by a visit to the men's room. As water trickled over the lenses of my glasses, I realized I'd have to come up with something else.

"Uh, I had to run down to the car."

"Why?"

Suddenly all my romantic charm came out in a classic response that every woman longs to hear: "Well, uh, my nose has been really stopped up, and I needed to get my nasal spray." (*Nasal spray!* Are you kidding me?)

"That's funny," she said. "You gave me your nasal spray earlier; I have it right here in my purse."

Busted!

I wondered if I should take the nasal spray and use it and then ask her to marry me. Or maybe try to explain about the park and my original plan, and the rain, and well, how we got to the nasal spray. Thankfully, I didn't!

Instead, I took her hands in mine, looked in her eyes, and quoted a passage from Ruth in the Bible: "'Don't ask me to leave you and turn back. Wherever you go, I will go; wherever you live, I will live. Your people will be my people, and your God will be my God. Wherever you die, I will die, and there I will be buried'"[1] (Ruth 1:16–17).

Then I walked around the table, dropped to one knee, and asked, "Lori, will you be my date for life? Will you marry me?"

People in the restaurant were watching us by now. This klutzy, dripping-wet guy was proposing to the calm, beautiful, bewildered-looking woman before him. I didn't care what anyone thought—anyone except Lori. In that moment there was only one word I wanted to hear—"yes."

I stopped breathing, and then she said it. Softly but clearly, this astonishing woman said, "Yes!" After Lori responded, I can't remember much of what happened. I was too awed by the realization that, despite all my faults and all my character flaws and my teal green Civic, she said, "Yes!"

That ridiculous, wonderful moment started a vibrant commitment between Lori and me, one filled with many ups and a few downs. We made a lifelong promise to each other that has continued to grow and develop. Every day we come to know new aspects of each other. We face conflict and work through it together. We grow in intimacy. We have been blessed with fantastic children and ponder how in the world we will parent them. Our marriage is far from effortless, but it is more than worth it.

No wonder then that when God wanted to illustrate the passionate intensity of His relationship with us, He chose marriage. And perhaps what's truly startling is that He didn't introduce this marriage with a fairy-tale story of the perfect, innocent princess and her Prince Charming. No, He chose a story that seems more at home on *Desperate Housewives,* a relationship that's completely peculiar and fractured—the marriage of the prophet Hosea and the prostitute Gomer.

AN UNTOLD LOVE STORY

My hunch is you haven't heard a lot about Hosea and Gomer. It's an odd story and certainly one that is hard to wrap our minds around. And let's just admit up front that Gomer's name adds to the offbeat vibe. I immediately think of Gomer Pyle—"Surprise, surprise surprise!"—but it's just a cultural difference. Even though our society celebrates love stories, this one is quite a stretch.

We're naturally drawn to movies such as *Pride and Prejudice* or *Notting Hill,* to name two of my wife's favorites, even if they leave us in tears. We cheered at the power of love triumphing in *Sleepless in Seattle.* We were charmed by a Hollywood fairy tale in *Pretty Woman.* We laughed through films such as *Crazy, Stupid, Love* and *Definitely, Maybe.*

And sometimes, the power of love sneaks up on us. Who could forget *Up?* This is a cartoon, for goodness' sake, but I cried twice when I first saw it. And then I teared up again the next day just thinking about the old man's love for his wife. I may have to surrender my man card for that!

In the Bible, there are scores of famous (and infamous) couples and the powerful love they shared. From Adam and Eve, to Jacob and Rachel (and Leah), Abraham and Sarah, David and Bathsheba, Samson and Delilah—lots of very intense bonds. Yet out of all the thousands of love stories, nobody has ever made a hit movie out of the story line of Hosea. (*Pretty Woman* doesn't even come close.)

Hosea, whose name means "salvation," had a unique role as a prophet of God. Unique in large part because God asked Hosea to do something He never asked anyone to do before (or after). He asked the prophet to marry a prostitute. Yep, you read that right. Not a *former* prostitute, but a full-fledged, card-carrying active prostitute. It definitely sounds insane. *Ludicrous.* It is. And that's the point—it compels us to notice God's divine obsession with His children.

Check it out: "When the Lord first began speaking to Israel through Hosea, he said to him, 'Go and marry a prostitute, so that some of her children will be conceived in prostitution'" (Hosea 1:2). Now, if I'm Hosea, I'm thinking I must have had too much of something with dinner the night before— "You want me to do what, Lord?" He must have thought, "My prophetic network server must be down because that is not a message I ever expected to hear from God. Surely that's not what He said."

And it got worse. Not only marry a prostitute, but if that isn't bizarre enough, she will have *children* that were conceived from her continued prostitution. And you, Hosea, Mr. Prophet Whose

Name Means Salvation, get to hold this happy little family together. *"Uh, God, can we talk about this?"*

YOU WANT ME TO DO WHAT?

Now, a little background info seems to be in order. Hosea was the spokesperson for God during desperate times. As God continued to watch and interact with the people of Israel, He was devastated to see His people turning their backs on Him and worshiping false gods. Whether it was a golden calf or a stone carving they made themselves, or one of the false gods they encountered in their many military skirmishes with neighboring tribes, they consistently looked everywhere else for the connection only God could provide.

Now in the grand scope of God's divine plan, He had already tried talking to them, rescuing them from slavery in Egypt, leading them to a new prosperous homeland, and establishing rules for them. But no matter how He demonstrated His love and concern for them, it didn't seem to matter. The Israelites continued to do their own thing. Over and over again.

God was distraught about it. So not only did He want His spokesman Hosea to deliver a message, but He wanted Hosea to speak from the same perspective of pain and frustration He felt. God explains His reason for commanding Hosea to marry a prostitute since "this will illustrate how Israel has acted like a prostitute by turning against the LORD and worshiping other gods" (Hosea 1:2).

Throughout history, some interpreters have tried to soften the story of Hosea. They have suggested Hosea was just having a vision to illustrate a point. Surely God wouldn't have literally asked him to do this. Yet this isn't taking the text in its straightforward context. Nor is that very comforting. Is it any less scandalous if God gave Hosea visions of this kind of marriage to teach us a lesson?

Either way we are confronted with something way beyond a Hallmark card. We are faced with a God who is more drastic than we are comfortable with. As I read the text, it seems clear this is a request to do the unthinkable, not figuratively but literally. If God wanted to domesticate the story, He could have told us so in the Bible, having the prophet deliver a disturbing parable instead of living out a painful reality. For my theological two cents, we are left to view this as a historical event.

As irrational, unexpected, and painful as it may seem to us, God is so passionate about us that He commanded Hosea to engage in a marriage that would crush his heart, just as God's heart had been crushed. While there may be many decisions and actions of God that seem beyond our ability to fathom, this one is up there with the time God told Abraham to sacrifice his son Isaac on a makeshift altar on a mountaintop. Faithful man that he was, Abraham prepared to do what God required, and God provided a ram for Abe to sacrifice instead, much to everyone's (especially Isaac's!) relief.

Such a sacrifice became a kind of dress rehearsal for the ultimate sacrifice God Himself would make many generations later. He would send His son, Jesus, to die nailed to a piece of wood between two thieves for the sake and salvation of all His people for all of time. God clearly has a divine obsession with us, His children. And measures we would consider outrageous, to say the least, are not beyond His limit to get His point across.

Such is the case with our main man here. Hosea marries

Gomer. By common cultural practices of the day, she may not have had much to do with it. Hosea would have worked out the arrangement with her father, who was likely thankful to have someone want to marry his tarnished daughter. No doubt she would have been an embarrassment to the family.

So for the first time in the Old Testament, the marriage metaphor is explicitly introduced and viscerally demonstrated. God makes it clear this metaphor was not just a figure of speech, a poetic comparison forged in a precious moment. Hosea's marriage to Gomer is now a lived-out, flesh-and-blood story of God's journey with His people.

From this point on in the Bible, marriage becomes a common stock image that symbolizes God's relationship with people.[2] In the New Testament, both Paul and John draw on the image of marriage to describe God's bond with us.[3] This finds its culmination at the wedding celebration in heaven: "Let us be glad and rejoice, and let us give honor to him. For the time has come for the wedding feast of the Lamb, and his bride has prepared herself" (Revelation 19:7). Here the lamb refers to Jesus, and bride is the community of believers, the church.

The marriage comparison not only introduces the book of Hosea, but is the foundation of the story line through the first three chapters as we move back and forth between Hosea's relationship with his wife, Gomer, and God's relationship with His people.

LET'S MAKE A DEAL

Hosea makes it clear God is not pursuing us *only* to convert us to a bunch of religious practices, but to lead us into a loving relationship with Him—not unlike marriage. This is an important distinction and leads to other questions which continue to resonate sharply for us today: What is Christianity really all about? Is it a religion or a relationship?

Sometimes Christianity can feel like an old organized religion, just another ball-and-chain dragging people down and forcing them to conform to socially acceptable standards. You've probably heard people say such things as, "Organized religion is for ignorant people," or even, "Organized religion and the church are human creations; Jesus didn't start a church and so I don't need any of that nonsense."

The main difference between "religion" and "relationship" is our *approach* or *attitude*. It has less to do with whether or not Christianity is organized or structured, and more to do with what we expect to get out of it and how we go about it. James writes, "Pure and genuine religion in the sight of God the Father means caring for orphans and widows in their distress and refusing to let the world corrupt you" (James 1:27). So there is such a thing as good religion that cultivates and restores both our association with God and the people who need help in our culture. When I use the term "religion," however, I'm talking about the not-so-good religion that reduces faith to ritual acts of devotion done for the wrong reason.

Religion in this sense approaches God as one might approach a car salesman for a transaction. The salesman wants to get as much out of you for as little as possible, and you want to get as much out of him for as little as possible. You both negotiate and compromise, passing notes with final amounts, until you reach an agreement that satisfies you both. Once you have completed the negotiations, you are both under certain obligations to each other—usually you are obligated to pay the salesman money, and he is obligated to give you keys and a vehicle to drive off the lot.

This is how religion approaches God. It says God wants certain things from us—our time, money, attention, worship—you get the idea. We want certain things from God, too—a successful job, good health, a happy marriage, a nice house, the latest cars, and more. We do stuff for God, such as praying, going to church, and giving money when we have to, and we expect Him to do certain things for us, such as providing us with a well-paying job and a healthy family.

Or maybe material blessings aren't what we're after. Maybe what we want from God are forgiveness and eternal life. So if we do all the right things in this life, then we'll have our mansion in heaven in the next. Now certainly none of these things are bad in themselves—a good job, happy family, forgiveness, and eternal life. But if our approach is still that we have done certain things for God, so He is obligated to do certain things for us, such as forgive us or dump the blessings truck, then we are still approaching God with that same religious car salesman attitude. Instead of selling cars or life insurance, God is selling forgiveness and eternal life insurance.

With this approach, we do things not out of love, but in order to negotiate with God—to put Him in our debt, to broker a deal. Of course, there are some major problems with this kind of viewpoint. The Bible says God owns everything since He made it all, so negotiating with God is like borrowing a lawnmower from your neighbor and then trying to sell it back to him.

The religious approach distorts our picture of who God is—His character, His personality, His passion. It gives us a picture of a god who is reluctant to give us things, who grinds us down

with constant ongoing negotiations and adherence to the minu-
tiae of a legally binding contract. (Think of all that fine print on
your phone service contract!) He gives us forgiveness and eternal
life only because He needs things from us and must barter with
us. This God is stingy, petty, capricious, and indifferent. He is not
the living God we see in the Bible and in the lives of so many
people who know Him.

In many ways, religion is the more accessible, perhaps even
attractive, approach because it is often human-centered—what
we can get out of God and what we must do to get it. But I'm
suggesting—in large part based on what I see in the book of
Hosea—that relationship is the more fulfilling approach because
it is God-centered—it's about how God *loves* us.

RUNNING HOME

So what does it mean to approach God with a relationship mind-
set then? The "relationship" approach radically challenges the
"salesman" picture of God. You don't want a relationship with
your car salesman and he doesn't want a relationship with you,
unless of course it will help him make the sale or if you need a
lot of cars. But true Christianity is different and upends this concept of God as supernatural salesman.

He's no longer a pitchman trying to sell us something; He's
a personal God trying to have a life with us. The relationship
approach undermines the religious sales contract notion and explains that God created us because He loves us and wants a
relationship with us; He redeemed us through the life and death
of Jesus because He loves us and wants a relationship with us; He

gives us eternal life because He loves us and wants an eternal relationship with us.

The reality is, so many of us continue to run from God both inside and outside the church. Maybe it's because we're expecting Him to be that angry cop or canny car salesman when He catches up to us. Maybe it's because others claiming to know and represent Him left us angry and deeply hurt, wary of religion like a dog that's kicked to the curb. Fear may keep us on the run because if we fully surrender to God, He might make us do a lot of things we don't want to do—such as give away some of our time or resources or go door-to-door carrying tracts or move to some foreign country as a missionary.

However, the scandalous story of Hosea and Gomer, and God's explicit explanation that their love depicts how He feels toward us, cannot be dismissed or explained within the confines of lifeless religion. No, what we see in Hosea is raw and relentless, unbridled and unkempt, a love that defies all logic and beats all odds.

The gospel of Hosea is this: No matter what we do, no matter how sinful we are, God pursues us, romances us, stalks us, and stakes us out in a radical grace based in Himself. When we run away from Him, God still pursues us. He comes after us. He calls us. And even when we are full of pain and hurt, He can still find and heal us.

I know because in addition to my own life, I've seen it happen time after time in the lives of so many others. My friend Randy was a pastor for eighteen years before he walked away from all of it. He and his wife, Joanne, had given all their attention and energy to their church. After running hard for years, leading women's ministry and caring for three young children at home, Joanne hit a wall and was diagnosed with clinical depression.

While she was trying to get well, which included some time in hospitals, their church's leaders were terribly concerned—not about Joanne really, but that one of their pastors' families would look less than perfect. One Sunday, Joanne went down for prayer at the end of the service and was quickly intercepted. The leaders didn't want anyone knowing there was a problem with a pastor's wife. They encouraged Randy to keep silent and just fake it at church so that no one would know.

After Joanne spent several months in the hospital, one nightmare led to another. Feeling alone and isolated and vulnerable, she met a fellow patient, and in their pain and confusion, they started a short-lived affair with a very long-lasting residue.

Depression was bad enough, but now an affair? When the church leaders found out about her affair, they panicked and immediately removed Randy from his position. From Randy's perspective, his best friend and senior pastor, along with their church family, turned their backs on him when he needed them the most. After all, he had done nothing deserving termination.

In a time when he and his family needed the support, comfort, and the love of God, his church fired him and divulged private details of their lives to defend the decision. Needless to say, my friends were devastated. They felt abandoned by the people that were supposed to love them and by God because these were supposedly His people. Randy told God what he thought of His people and just checked out.

Can you blame him? Maybe those who represent God have betrayed you as well. You know what it is to carry the pain and frustration of empty promises or harmful gossip for years. The fact that nobody spoke up or tried to make things right, or even cared enough to check on you, still stings. Obviously, Randy's church blew it. My mom always used to say that if the church were perfect, there wouldn't be any people in it. All I could think when I heard Randy's story was how much of an understatement this was for his experience.

Randy and Joanne were exhausted. The formula they had bought into had failed. So they ran from God and His church. Joanne kept getting sicker and sicker and Randy just got madder and madder. For the next four years, Joanne was in and out of the hospital while Randy struggled in the role of single dad and caretaker.

About eight years after they left their church, they felt like they hit rock bottom when Randy lost his job. In order to find a new job, they moved to Las Vegas. Joanne took some classes and started working as an EMT. After so many rides in ambulances, she wanted to overcome her fear of them. She began to recover through this new purpose and a sense of God in her life that had nothing to do with what she'd experienced at their old church. She was good at serving people, many with the same kind of physical and emotional needs as herself, and this purpose helped her battle her depression.

Meanwhile, Randy grew more and more bitter. When Joanne suggested they consider trying to find a church, he said, "Not a chance in hell. I'm never going back to church." But eventually he became so desperate that he caved. Later he would tell me that he knew God was working on his heart, reminding Randy of His love even in the midst of such pain and turmoil.

Randy and Joanne walked into Central Christian Church, the church where I serve as pastor in the Las Vegas area, and heard an unexpected message from the platform: "It's okay to not be okay. You don't have to have things worked out." They were both in tears, wrecked because they were not okay and hadn't been okay for some time. They were emotionally out of breath from their constant running. All the anger, bitterness, and hatred toward people had changed them. The depression, fear, and uncertainty—it all was summed up in the realization that they were *so* not okay, but they could be accepted anyway.

After that weekend, they started to attend faithfully, and for about two years, they just soaked it all in. They healed. When their kids started getting involved in youth group, Randy said that he forbade them from telling anyone their dad was a former pastor. He just wanted to keep testing the waters, seeing if this kind of place and this way of knowing God were for real.

Our video team then asked them to be part of a video in which people would share their stories in bite-sized headlines. Randy's was simply: BURNED BY THE CHURCH. RESTORED IN JESUS CHRIST. Joanne's: ABUSE, ADULTERY, AND SUICIDE. HEALED, FORGIVEN, AND ALIVE. This marked a moment of true freedom for Randy and Joanne, but one that came after running for a very long time.

Eighteen years serving God as a pastor. Eight years hurt, angry, and on the run. Through it all, God didn't quit on them. He didn't walk away. He drew them back to Himself. And miraculously, they didn't quit on each other. Today, Randy and Joanne are back in ministry and even serving in their former denomination. They know as well as anyone that God is all about us relating to Him and helping others experience Him. They know a God who keeps coming no matter how far we run.

IT'S COMPLICATED

Like Randy and Joanne, Hosea and Gomer's relationship was also complicated and broken down. All the drama flying around surely created tensions and layers that are hard to fathom unless you're living them. The resentment and frustration from such a messed-up beginning surely took its toll. Gomer continued to be unfaithful but Hosea didn't give up, and he didn't check out. He kept pursuing her, kept loving her, no matter how much she betrayed that love. Just as God keeps pursuing us.

This truth is what the religion perspective misses—*God is all about relationship*. Consider the world of dating. Thanks to social media, we're all constantly connected. Before you connect with someone over dinner, you do a background check and scope him or her out online. The next step is "just talking." It's casual, just a text here and there, a friend request or a message through social media. Then you move to hanging out. Now you're out together in the real world, first with friends and then just you two. Coffee or lunch meetings happen, but you're not dating. You're just hanging out.

From here, things can go back to "just talking" or they may move forward to exclusive dating and then one day marriage. If you decide to keep hanging out indefinitely, you'll find yourself in this in-between place where you're not really just hanging out and you're not officially dating exclusively. When people ask what's going on with your relationship, you reply, "It's Complicated." There are more and more people wandering in the "It's Complicated" stage. So many, in fact, there's an official Facebook relationship status called "It's Complicated."

There are a lot of people in the "It's Complicated" status of their faith as well.

After you've been a Christian for years, maybe your faith has stalled out. At previous seasons you grew and were excited about your faith and learning all you could about God. Those days seem like the distant past. A loss or crisis has robbed you of your once simple faith. You're a believer stuck in a rut or stuck in a moment that longs to move forward, but is riddled with doubts. It's complicated.

Other Christians or a church may have hurt you, talked about you behind your back, or burned you. Their actions sent you on a long path in many directions. You're both ready and terrified to come home to God and the faith community, but you're having a hard time trusting as well. It's complicated.

Living a double life is something you never thought you'd do; yet perhaps you are here. You pray and even go to church, but you know your lifestyle is in complete contradiction to your faith. Frayed and worn out, you keep giving in to temptation, but you also keep one foot in the faith. If people really knew what was going on, they would be more than a little baffled. Heck, you're baffled. It's complicated.

Or maybe your connection with God is like a married couple that no longer goes out, no longer communicates, and just lives together like two divorced people under the same roof. The contract is in place and the duties are performed, but deep down you know you were made for more than this. It's complicated.

God desires for us to update our status from "It's Complicated" to devoted "Marriage." Not a marriage that fits in one's worst stereotype, but one that leads to new life and renewed hope. In movies and sitcoms, guys cringe at making a commitment as girlfriends seek to tie them down. That's not how real love works. Both people want more of the other, to grow together, to know each other at deeper, richer, sweeter levels of intimacy. God wants more than halfhearted dating; He's proposing something else. He's calling us to exclusive commitment.

All of history has been moving us forward toward that moment when a loud voice comes from the throne of heaven, saying, "Look, God's home is now among his people! He will live with them, and they will be his people. God himself will be with them" (Revelation 21:3). When the end comes, John says, "We will see him as he really is" (1 John 3:2), and Paul says, "Now we see things imperfectly as in a cloudy mirror, but then we will see everything with perfect clarity. All that I know now is partial and incomplete, but then I will know everything completely, just as God now knows me completely" (1 Corinthians 13:12).

The Bible includes the promise that we "will see his face, and his name will be written on [our] foreheads" (Revelation 22:4). So much of what God does for us is for the purpose of this relationship. Religion and relationship often say the same thing, but the fundamental difference is *orientation*. One is sterile, self-serving, and dead; the other is vibrant, beautiful, and life-giving.

It may feel complicated in your life right now, but it doesn't have to be. As we'll see, God's love and grace are enough to pull you through whatever you face.

Go ahead, update your status.

CHAPTER TWO

→

passionate pursuit

Every man who knocks on the door of a
brothel is looking for God.

—*G. K. Chesterton*

my friend annie Lobert grew up in a small town in the Mid-
west, a pretty girl who made good grades, went to church with
her family, and stayed out of trouble. If you saw her today here
in the suburbs of Las Vegas, you might mistake her for any other
trendy mom. A charming woman in her late thirties who radi-
ates a zeal for life and a fervent love for God, Annie has traveled
a painful, circuitous route in her search to know Him and find
healing.

You see, in between her small-town roots and current life here
in the burbs of Vegas, Annie endured a roller-coaster ride of alcoholism, drug addiction, and sexual promiscuity that few can
imagine. She went from middle-class good girl to high-class call
girl as part of a slow, gradual descent into the darkness of her
own doubt, fear, and pain. Like so many people in the sex-trade

industry, Annie was sexually abused by a family friend when she was just eight years old.

Consequently, she never fully felt loved or valued. This act of abuse lowered her self-esteem to the degree that she became desperate for love and willing to do anything to get it. Even though her family attended church, it never occurred to her to look to God for the kind of love she wanted. In church, they talked about this loving, kind, and gracious God, but Annie just couldn't believe what they were saying was true. She assumed that if God were real, which she doubted, then He must be really angry with her. She couldn't imagine how He could love someone who had been through something like she had experienced. Additionally, her strict upbringing contributed to her rebellion as a party girl during her teen years.

So Annie looked for comfort where she could find it, in the arms of a bad boy more than willing to use a good girl for his own desires. At eighteen, she fell head over heels in love and willingly gave her body away for the first time. It wasn't long, however, until she discovered her boyfriend was cheating on her, and her already cracked heart felt like it shattered into a dozen pieces. For a brief period, the intoxicating feelings of her infatuation had made her feel good about herself. So she set out on a quest to find more ways to ease the pain that continued to swirl inside her.

A string of boyfriends led to one-night stands with guys she picked up in clubs, which included lots of drinking, drugging, and partying. During this season of her life, Annie found herself raped by a man while she was barely conscious, the first of many such assaults on her body and soul. While her anguish only intensified, she became more committed to finding a way to be loved, to escape the horror her life was quickly becoming.

Hungry for acceptance, she nevertheless continued looking for love in all the wrong places. She found when she gave herself sexually to men, for those brief moments, she felt "wanted" and "needed." Finally, she became so desperate for male attention that she went on vacation to Hawaii, only to start working as an exotic dancer and prostitute. Then she moved back to Minnesota, where she met a man who swept her off her feet, who said he sincerely loved her and wanted to take care of her. Not realizing it at the time, Annie had actually met an undercover abusive pimp whose sole intention was to sex-traffic her and other girls for profit. After a few months of working in Minnesota, the desire for more money led her to Vegas. She envisioned getting in, making enough money to go to college, and then getting out, a dream that quickly became a nightmare.

Her first night in Las Vegas was the night she found out that her trusted friend and lover had now become her guerrilla pimp. For more than a decade, Annie was enslaved to the lifestyle of prostitution physically, emotionally, spiritually, and mentally. Even though Annie chose the lifestyle of the sex industry as a career, like many other ladies, she was eventually coerced by this abusive pimp into a dark life of sex trafficking with no clear way out.

The glamour and glimmer of the Las Vegas strip had lured Annie into a lifestyle that found her staying up for days on end, getting so drunk and so high that she would pass out on the floor of her home. Alone with her drugs, wine, and cigarettes, and wrapped in a mink coat, she remembers rocking back and forth in the corner of her bedroom, terrified of the past but more afraid of the future. How in the world did she get here?

When she first arrived in Sin City, she used to pity the people she encountered who were so strung out, desperately scrambling and searching on the floor for a small piece of "rock" so they could sustain their high for just another few minutes. Now she had become that person, trapped in a vicious cycle of numbness to escape the painful reality constantly threatening to erupt inside her heart. Days bled into nights, weeks into years, and Annie found herself trapped in a hellish existence with no exit in sight.

Aware of the vacancy in her soul, she flirted with a garden variety of spiritual practices and belief systems, including Buddhism, Wicca, New Ageism—even vampirism! But nothing filled that cold, dark cavern of pain inside her. She was beyond disappointment at who she had become, at how she allowed control of her life to slip through her fingers. Finally, she was as low as she could go.

WHAT'S YOUR NAME?

Perhaps, like Annie Lobert, Gomer also thought she could outrun the pain of her past. She, too, took a long time before she hit rock bottom. She continued to live a double life, even after she was shown real love by her husband. Given the opportunity to experience a loving home and a caring family, Gomer continued to pursue her old habits.

Similarly, God's people, the Israelites, were making a parallel journey. He offered them a spiritual home, His protection, and security. Yet they continued to go their own way, pursing old idols and chasing counterfeit gods. They were in denial about the mess they were making of their lives so God tried to jolt them back to reality through the story of Hosea and Gomer.

God is still hoping to shake us up with their romance. Too often we keep avoiding, keep shucking and jiving away from the real issues of our lives, reluctant to stop and face the truth about who we are and what we need. God desires for us to be faithful to Him just as Hosea had hoped his bride would be to him.

And certainly Hosea had some hopeful moments, such as when he and Gomer had their first child, a son. This wonderful occasion should have been filled with joy, but in their case it became a living example of the rift in their marriage. God tells them to name the child "Jezreel," which means "God scatters" (Hosea 1:4). While it wasn't uncommon for the name of a prophet's child to be symbolic for the prophet's message, Jezreel wasn't exactly the name any parent would choose for his or her child.

Basically, this name connotes bloodshed and violence, catastrophe and crisis. Some scholars say it would be the equivalent of naming a child "Auschwitz" or "Hiroshima"[1] today. Can you imagine the expression on people's faces if you introduced your infant son as "World Trade Center"? The response would be shock, disbelief, even disgust.

Not long after the birth of their son, Hosea and Gomer have a daughter, who unfortunately fares no better than her big brother in the name department. God tells Hosea to name his daughter "Lo-ruhamah," which means "not loved" (Hosea 1:6). Imagine Hosea going around the house calling his children Jezreel (God scatters) and Lo-ruhamah (not loved)!

I remember holding my daughter, our firstborn, on the day of her birth and feeling overwhelmed with love for her. In that moment of cradling her in my arms, I resolved to do anything to keep her safe, to take care of her and protect her. I called out her name for the first time, "Emma," and it was a beautiful sound for us both to hear. Oh, the effort Lori and I had put into choosing that name. Nine months of baby name books, website searches, and disagreements. Nine months of trying to anticipate any terrible nicknames playground bullies could create. Emma: to us, it was loveliness, innocence, and gentleness.

As much as I'm sure Hosea and Gomer loved their children, they couldn't even speak to their son or whisper their daughter's name without a painfully harsh reminder from God. Their third child, another boy, is named Lo-ammi, which means "not my people" (Hosea 1:9). It dramatically represents a fracture between God and His people. He called them to be His special people from among the nations, and yet their behavior is no different from that of the people in the surrounding lands.

At this point you might be feeling like God is just being cruel. I mean, come on, commanding parents to name their kids these names seems tantamount to endorsing a form of child abuse. Wouldn't we call Child Protective Services today? Yes, it is extreme and it's meant to bother us, but we'll see there is more to God than meets the eye here.

The first chapter of Hosea reads like a horrible, painful, breakup letter from God. He's so disturbed by the persistent fickleness of human hearts that He sounds like He can't take it anymore. Basically, God allows us to see Him in a way that's shockingly transparent—as a jilted, brokenhearted lover.

THE THINGS WE DO FOR LOVE

Now understandably, love makes you do some pretty crazy things. When Lori and I were dating and living in different cities,

I spent every cent I had on phone bills. We once sat for hours rolling quarters, nickels, and dimes to pay the bills. I shelled out hundreds of dollars, often just to hear the smallest details of her day, but the cost didn't matter to me. I had to keep calling her. It felt like I would die if I didn't hear her voice every day, ideally for hours at a time.

Similarly, I'd drive ridiculously long distances just to spend an hour with her. I even started wearing dark green shirts all the time because she said it was "my color." Before I met her, I didn't even know I had a color! But I would have worn neon pink every day if it had made her happy. If you've ever been in love, then you know how it makes you act a little crazy.

Part of the insanity was the constant cycle I saw many of my friends get into. They'd fall in love, break up for some reason, find life unbearable without the other person, and then get back together, only to repeat the cycle three months later. Crazy, right? Yet we basically see God act this way as He threatens to break off His relationship with the people He loves.

Just as God acts like He's breaking up with the people of Israel, He then looks ahead and affirms He can't stop loving them: "Yet the time will come when Israel's people will be like the sands of the seashore—too many to count! Then, at the place where they were told, 'You are not my people,' it will be said, 'You are children of the living God'" (Hosea 1:10).

This "I love them, I love them not" yo-yoing continues back and forth throughout the book of Hosea. In no other book do we find both some of the most graphic language of judgment sandwiched in between surprisingly poetic language of love and comfort. If God really didn't care about His children, then He wouldn't even bother telling them how upset He was! He would just abandon them to the consequences of their own selfishness. He'd just pull back and go away and move on. But like a jealous lover, He cares too much.

MEETING IN THE MESS

Hosea shows us that God pursues us no matter how big of a mess we may make in our running. I walked into Las Vegas's Caesars Palace with a friend when I was reminded of this. As he was talking to me, he paused mid-sentence and just threw up. Barf city. Vomito. Right there while I was looking at his face in the middle of a conversation. I've never seen anything like it to this day. (I know, this is the second time I've mentioned throwing up, but stay with me here. I promise I won't bring it up again!)

We took a few steps, and I said, "Are you going to be all right?"

He nodded and said, "I'm better now." Remembering there was a restroom close by in the other direction, we did an about-face and reversed course.

Then the gross evolved into the truly horrific. As if in slow motion, I watched as this lady walking briskly along slipped on the puddle my friend had just left. Both feet flew out from under her and she landed with a thud—splat!—on her back in a pool of nastiness. It was just...*wrong*. The poor woman never saw it coming.

Isn't that the way life seems sometimes? You're just walking along and all of a sudden both feet are up in the air, you land on your backside, and find yourself right in the middle of a major mess. Perhaps, like this unfortunate lady, one not even of your own making.

Many times we don't realize we're walking into a mess until

it is too late. It's hard to imagine sitting amid nastiness and not recognizing it, but it happens all the time. I've sat in the mess of a ho-hum faith that had become little more than trying to keep up appearances for other people. I've remained in the mess of my own selfishness and sinful habits that I hid behind a reputation as a church guy and pastor. And I've wallowed in the mess of trusting in my own righteousness rather than God's.

No matter what our motive or how we attempt to justify it, sin is an enormous puddle of yuck separating us from God and the new life He invites us into. And it is exhausting because we're created for so much more. We don't always fully perceive the junk we remain in, but imagine coming up on somebody sitting in it and trying to help them up. Now imagine such a person looking up at you and saying, "No, thanks. I'm good. I don't need any help."

What kind of mess are you facing right now? It could be the wreckage of uncontrolled spending and debt or the turmoil of bitterness toward a family member or friend. It could be the chaos of anger issues or functional alcoholism or binging and purging with food. Maybe it's the confusion from seeking romance to fill a need only God can fill. God enthusiastically wants to be able to help us face our sin and discover why we were created. And when we choose to remain a mess rather than become His masterpiece, we arouse profound emotions in God.

AN EMOTIONAL GOD

We see this emotional aspect of God elsewhere in the Bible, but Hosea exposes the way God communicates to us at a heart level. In the Bible, God often discloses Himself in very human and emotional terms so we might further understand Him. In fact, there are hundreds of references to the emotions of God, most of them in the Old Testament.

Have you ever struggled with the idea that God is emotional? Some people tend to disclaim His emotions or explain them away. Yet God wants us to relate to Him as He really is, and He shows He can genuinely grieve, His heart full of pain. Since God made us in His image, we should assume our emotions are reflective of His, even though ours are subject to sin while His are not. Put your seat belt on and consider the range of God's emotions through a small sampling of verses from Hosea:

> But now bring charges against Israel—your mother—for she is no longer my wife, and I am no longer her husband. Tell her to remove the prostitute's makeup from her face and the clothing that exposes her breasts. Otherwise, I will strip her as naked as she was on the day she was born. I will leave her to die of thirst, as in a dry and barren wilderness (2:2–3).

> I will show love to those I called "Not loved." And to those I called "Not my people," I will say, "Now you are my people." And they will reply, "You are our God!" (2:23).

> My fury burns against you. How long will you be incapable of innocence? (8:5).

> My heart is torn within me, and my compassion overflows (11:8).

> I will heal you of your faithlessness; my love will know no bounds, for my anger will be gone forever (14:4).

Does all this strike you as a little odd for God to say? Are you surprised at how engaged He is in the relationship? Some people, especially men, often struggle to share their emotions, but here we see God has no problem pouring them out everywhere. At some point reading this, you may start to feel uncomfortable, like you're getting a little TMI (too much information).

Prophetic books such as Hosea often seem melodramatic as emotions, judgments, anger, love, and compassion seem to fly all over the page. Many believers just shut themselves off from these texts because they are hard to grasp and make sense of; yet there is so much here. Yes, it is disturbing to read of God punishing or judging His people. It is frightening to behold His anger. These books and each individual passage need to be held up to the context of the entire Bible to get the full story of God, but they are here for a reason. I'm never so humbled or grounded as when I read prophets such as Hosea and reflect on both my sin and God's affection. All these emotions exist in God as a reflection of His deep concern.

Another passage that reveals a striking part of God's emotional response to us is in Isaiah: "Then God will rejoice over you as a bridegroom rejoices over his bride" (62:5). When Lori walked down the aisle on our wedding day, I was filled with so much joy I thought I would explode. She looked angelic in a simple but elegant ivory dress. She had saved every rose I had given her while we dated, and she had many of them dried and bundled into the bouquet she carried. Her smile was infectious (and a little nervous). I just couldn't get over how fortunate I was to be marrying this woman. Isaiah says this is how God views us, His people.

What a remarkable image! As a believer, this applies to *you*! Neither your sin, your mistakes, your past, nor your present disqualifies you. God rejoices over you, beaming like a groom on his wedding day! His love and sheer excitement toward you are beyond boundaries. His happiness over you is sky-high. He's filled with goodwill, compassion, and generosity. He's imagining a fantastic future with you. As John Piper put it, "When God does good to his people it is not so much like a reluctant judge showing kindness to a criminal whom he finds despicable (though that analogy has truth in it); it is like a bridegroom showing affection to his bride."[2]

In order to relate to us with such depth and intensity, God also enters into our pain. One passage about God's goodness and compassion that has always spoken to me reveals His divine empathy: "In all *their* distress *he* too was distressed" (Isaiah 63:9 NIV). In the original Hebrew language, a form of the same word is used to describe our distress and God's own. Yes, our distress can involve feelings that God doesn't feel, such as helplessness, anxiety, fear, and uncertainty. But plainly God intends for us to see a similarity between our emotional distress and His own.

ANGER MANAGEMENT

Everybody likes to hear about the affection of God, but another emotion God reveals is anger. This one is a little harder to swallow. Yet the emotion of God's anger weaves its way through Hosea. It makes sense on paper, right? Because God is holy and perfect, He's upset by our imperfect choices and behavior. But how do we get our minds around all this anger without reducing God to somebody who needs anger management courses? How do we reconcile the God who rejoices over us with the one who expresses anger? It is helpful to realize that anger is not intrinsically part of who God is in the same way that love defines Him. God is love at all times; He never ceases to be love (1 John 4:8). His anger is an expression of His love and holiness when confronted with sin, with betrayal, with disobedience.

Holiness necessarily expresses anger when it is confronted by what is unholy. Although the love a husband has for his wife does not necessarily include anger, you better believe if another man threatens his wife, the love the husband has for her naturally gets expressed through anger toward her assailant. A mother's love for her children also doesn't necessarily involve anger, but if the kids are in danger, the mama bear claws instinctively show themselves.

We don't understand this aspect of God very well. We are not holy as God is holy, and so sometimes we do not get the natural reaction God expresses to our selfishness. This has actually increased my faith in the God of the Bible. If God were just some human creation made in our image, then I imagine He'd be presented as having nothing but warm and fuzzy feelings that make us feel comfortable. The God revealed in the Bible loves us way more than that, and His passion and holiness are more untamed than we can sometimes grasp.

I often hear Christians say God expresses much more of His anger in the Old Testament and much more of His love in the New Testament—maybe you've heard that, too. However, if you think about it, both God's love and His anger are present in both the Old and the New Testaments. They collide in the New Testament through Jesus' death on the cross. There had to be some way to atone for our wrongdoings so we could have affiliation with Him. Sacrificing His Son became the means to that end.

Another misconception we often hold emerges when we separate God and His emotions by saying God is full of anger while Jesus is full of love. Basically, it's the notion that Jesus is for us, but God is against us, the compassionate hero and His angry old man. Yet pitting Jesus and God against one another is not in line with what the Bible teaches. You're probably familiar with the best evidence to the contrary in John 3:16: "For *God loved* the world so much that he gave his one and only Son, so that everyone who believes in him will not perish but have eternal life." Both Jesus and God love humanity and are the same One.

JEALOUS EYES

Ever since my first day in preschool, I've spelled my name out loud. I have to. The first day of a new school year was always a challenge for me growing up. I'd always be at the back of the line and one of the last ones called. And last, but not least, "William Wilhit." I'd tell them no, it was "Wilhite," and though my first name is William, I go by my middle name, which is Jud.

They'd say, "Jude?"

"No, Jud: J-U-D."

They would always look down at their book and say, "I have Judson here."

I'd say, "That is my middle name, but my grandfather went by Jud, and that is what I go by: J-U-D."

Then they'd say, "Not two D's?"

"Nope, just one."

By then, I was totally embarrassed and the whole class was looking at me. Do you know how many things rhyme with Jud? A lot, and I was called all of them in elementary school...Mud,

Dud, Pud…. And yes, I've had "Poor Jud Is Dead" from *Oklahoma* sung to me more than a few times.

So I've navigated this name problem my whole life. I hear, "William Wilit, the doctor will see you now." Or, "Jude, your prescription is ready." At one point in college, one of our professors told students the meaning of their names in Hebrew. Students would tell him their names and he'd say, "That means, 'strong and mighty one.'" Or, "That means, 'warrior princess.'" I got all excited. I told him my name was Judson, and he said, "That means 'son of Jud.'" That's it! How utterly disappointing.

The only good thing about it is I know immediately when telemarketers are calling because they have no idea who I am. It is a good thing I know who I really am.

In Biblical times, a person's name and its meaning often defined them and foretold the story of their life. The fact that a person had multiple, contradictory names was not considered a problem, only an accurate indication of that person's complicated identity. So it's not surprising that we see so many unique and various names for God in the Scriptures. One that may trouble us the most can be found in Exodus 34, where we're told that God's name is Jealous.

Jealousy is commonly regarded as negative in our culture and associated with anger, envy, and a possessive, controlling love. The Biblical portrait of jealousy is far different, describing a God whose intense care is devoted to His people. He will accept nothing less than the best for those He loves.

To be jealous in His eyes, then, is to prevent His people from falling into the hands of anything that might divert their lives from Him. As J. I. Packer explains, "God's jealousy is not a compound of frustration, envy, and spite, as human jealousy so often is, but appears instead as a…praiseworthy zeal to preserve something supremely precious."[3] God is zealous to protect and preserve His place in our life. Because He is most highly prized and precious, He is protective of our devotion, not like some deviant stalker who means harm but as One who wants to jealously guard what is best.

God shows His jealousy by removing the satisfaction things can give, so that we seek satisfaction in Him. He may take away wealth or health or hobbies to shake us up. He may allow whatever we are trusting in ahead of Him to fail us and leave us with nothing but Him. He is jealous of our trust and our company.

Our difficulty with trying to understand the emotional dimension of God is that we are limited by our own human emotions. Ours may run the gamut and be influenced by our circumstances, medication, personality—even the weather! While God feels what we feel, His emotions never spin out of control.

Our God is not the hapless victim of circumstance. He is never caught unaware, nor do His emotions ever go off the rails. There is nothing beyond Him or bigger than Him that would cause Him to suffer. Rather, by relating with His people, He has deliberately made Himself vulnerable. He refuses to protect Himself from the frustrations and heartache that such an association might involve. He opens Himself up to rejection and suffering, but also to the joys and delights that cannot be experienced apart from such interactions. He longs to be loved for who He is and not just what He does for us.

FOR THE LOVE OF GOD

Hosea reveals that God's pursuit of us is incredibly passionate. Just imagine Hosea's emotions toward Gomer. They are married now and having kids, but she's still cheating. She's still slipping out and disappearing and giving herself to others. Hosea feels incredible hurt, betrayal, and anger, which are intimately connected to love and concern. More than anything, he wants her to stay home and love him freely as he loves her.

You may wonder if Hosea really loves Gomer in this way. After all, didn't God *command* Hosea to marry Gomer? Maybe all this proves is that Hosea loves God. Yet if Hosea didn't love Gomer beyond a mere obligation, the whole picture of God's love for us through their marriage would begin to break down. We can assume, based on God's own passionate response to us, that Hosea has come to truly love Gomer. Yes, there was the command of God and there was an arranged marriage, but the message of Hosea reveals there is an underlying love that goes deeper than surface duty.

As the months turn into years, Gomer keeps running, and Hosea keeps pursuing. She feels unlovable; Hosea keeps loving her. She feels as if Hosea should just let her go; this is who she is and what she does. Hosea sees who she can become and won't give up. She likely told him he was out of his mind to love her in the first place and now she's proven it, but he loves her just the same.

If we were retelling the story of Hosea and Gomer from a typical religious view, it might go something like this: "Then Gomer felt really bad. She promised to clean up her act, pledged never to sleep with other men, and after a few weeks of keeping her promise, Hosea started to visit her occasionally. After two months of good behavior, he let her move back into his house but watched her every move. Gomer did lots of good things to pay Hosea back and prove herself to him, and that helped change Hosea's mind. Over the next few years because she was so good, and lived a moral life, Hosea fully accepted her and began to love her again."

Religion may try to refine the story of Hosea and Gomer this way, but God doesn't. Hosea still loved her and pursued Gomer even without evidence of remorse or life change, just as God pursues us. He obviously doesn't wait for us to change and clean up our act before He pursues us. He doesn't care how terrible your past is, how many times you've screwed up, or how ashamed you feel in the dark desperation of your need. He keeps coming toward you in love.

Annie Lobert, whose story I told at the beginning of this chapter, hit rock bottom with nowhere else to turn and no one else to call on. With tears and mascara running down her face, Annie remembers crying out to God after all she'd done, "Where are you, God? I'm so mad at you, God! Why me? Why is this happening to me?" She knew she could no longer keep going this way, but she still couldn't see a way out.

Finally, after overdosing on a mix of cocaine, alcohol, and Xanax one night, she remembers taking another hit of coke and thinking she was going to die. She immediately felt a fierce pain in her chest and knew her young heart had reached its limit. As she fell to the ground, Annie felt her breathing slow down, sensed darkness all around her, and expected to die.

In her terror and desperation, she says it was all she could do to muster these words from her lips, "Jesus, I'm so sorry! Please forgive me! If you are real, God, please give me a second chance!" When she returned to consciousness many hours later, Annie knew Jesus had heard her cry and saved her life. In fact, she knew the confused, tortured young woman she had been did indeed die on the marble floor of her luxurious home. She felt like Lazarus returning from the dead, given her life back.

Annie kept the promise she made to God that night. She quit prostitution and got help for her alcohol and drug addictions. And as she grew stronger and started to experience the healing fullness of God's love, she knew God wanted her to help other women and men escape the darkness of the sex industry.

So Annie started a ministry called "Hookers for Jesus," a faith-based organization that addresses the realities of human sex trafficking, sexual violence, and exploitation linked to pornography and the sex industry. With a name inspired by Christ's invitation to become "fishers of men" (Matthew 4:19), Hookers for Jesus is passionate about seeing men and women break free from their pain—the life-threatening, soul-deadening pain that Annie lived through for eleven years.

Finally free, Annie now uses her story to let others know they are loved. Remembering how irrelevant and judgmental the church had felt to her throughout her life, Annie wants to make sure that every man and woman held captive by the sex industry hears of the freedom found in Christ. She wants to show them a community of Christians who love and support them the way God does, unconditionally and without judgment.

Maybe your sins don't seem so bad compared to someone like Annie or Gomer. God confronts us with extremes in Gomer's story to showcase His unexpected, jealous love. No matter where you find yourself right now, God is moved by you.

Have you ever considered how you stir the emotions of God? What He *feels* when He sees you? He isn't so removed that He doesn't care. Pause for a few moments and just imagine God smiling over you, rejoicing over you, celebrating you like a groom rejoices in his bride on their wedding day! Visualize God overflowing with compassion as He relates to you. Picture His love toward you knowing *no* bounds. Think about Him jealously protecting you and providing for you. See Him running toward you, pursuing you, welcoming your interaction with Him. Don't resist it and make excuses about how you're disqualified! This love is anchored in God's worthiness more than your own. Receive it and be rejuvenated by it in faith!

As you relate to God and surrender to Him, these are the kinds of emotions God has revealed He feels toward you. Let these images settle deep into your soul.

Stay awhile. Soak it in. Breathe. Close your eyes.

You are loved beyond words.

CHAPTER THREE

→

an affair to remember

> Every one of us is, even from his mother's
> womb, a master craftsman of idols.
>
> —*John Calvin*

growing up, did you ever stick a poster of someone you idolized on the wall in your room? Maybe Michael Jackson or Madonna or even Patrick Swayze from *Dirty Dancing*? Or maybe it was the best-selling poster of all time, the 1976 *Life* magazine cover featuring Farrah Fawcett? If that was before your time, maybe it was the Backstreet Boys, N Sync, Michael Jordan, Lance Armstrong, Britney Spears, or even Taylor Swift, who is currently plastered up in my daughter's room.

You might even be one of the "Beliebers," as the hardcore fans of teen sensation Justin Bieber call themselves. With numbers and intensity to rival the fan base of Elvis, the Beliebers will do just about anything to get close to Justin or to increase his fame. One young Bieber fan took a knife and carved JB I LOVE on her arm. An obsessed mom got a Justin Bieber tattoo on her lower back so her daughter could get backstage passes to his next concert. One fan even paid $683 for a water bottle from which Justin had taken a few sips.

Today we have celebrities with incredible talent and we have those who are famous for...being famous. From Bachelors to Kardashians, from Real Housewives to Iron Chefs, everyone clamors for their fifteen minutes in the spotlight, reveling in the attention, and in most cases, the money that accompanies it. In the ancient world, people elevated well-known kings and military leaders, but fame as we know it today is a product of our culture. And while I think having posters and enjoying certain performers or athletes is no big deal, it's important we remember who's at the center of our heart's devotion.

Are posters hanging in the room of your heart that capture your time and attention more than God?

SELLING YOURSELF SHORT

The issues with Hosea and Gomer's marriage would be right at home on a reality TV show today. Of course, they'd have to tame it down quite a bit just to air it! The problem was not Gomer's salacious past as a prostitute. Nor was it the adultery resulting from her return to other lovers. No, the problem we see in this woman's life screams of counterfeit things she's seeking to fill her life; it screams of idolatry.

It's not just another man she's in love with; it's the brief moments of significance, fake love, temporary pleasure, or personal power her actions produce. Gomer blatantly and openly sought out and maintained illicit affairs. She bore children with different fathers than her husband and remained about as indiscreet as a person can be. She said, along with God's people, "I'll run after other lovers and sell myself to them for food and water, for clothing of wool and linen, and for olive oil and drinks" (Hosea 2:5).

There's nothing romantic about her behavior here. Today we would call her a sex and love addict. Gomer's not having some clandestine affair with secret rendezvous in discreet locations. There's no paying with cash at out-of-the-way hotels or deleting racy text messages. She brazenly chases her lovers right out in public, going after them without shame, even trusting them to provide basic necessities like food and clothes for her. Talk about selling yourself short!

Can you imagine Hosea's hurt and frustration? One infidelity would crush any partner, but a repeat offender like Gomer must have destroyed this man of God who loved her. Was she even willing to try and make their marriage work? Did he have any hope she was open to change?

Knowing God uses their marriage to portray His own anguish makes the story even more poignant. Basically, through their lives, God pulls the curtain back and shows us His heart, saying in essence, *My people have betrayed me the same way. They prefer having spiritual affairs rather than honoring our commitment.* Like any devoted lover, He doesn't want to take second place to anything.

Naturally, we desire things to bring us joy, happiness, and significance. We are driven to search for these things and God has placed these desires in our hearts. He's not calling us to less pleasure but to *more*, a pleasure that is ultimately grounded in Him. Too often we expect more from romance, sex, money, comfort food, or hobbies than they were created to give. When we set our hearts ultimately on other things than God, we find they don't return what we were hoping they would. They actually return the opposite—emptiness, regret, bitterness, and disappointment.

Arthur Miller describes his marriage to Marilyn Monroe in his autobiography, *Timebends*. He talks of her slow descent into dependence on barbiturates, depression, growing paranoia, and hostility. He was afraid for her life. After a doctor was swayed to give her another shot so she could rest, Marilyn finally fell asleep. As Miller watched her sleep, he was moved to later write, "I found myself straining to imagine miracles. What if she were to wake and I were able to say, 'God loves you, darling,' and she were able to believe it! How I wished I still had my religion and she hers."[1] Beneath the layers of hurt and addiction remained an awareness that God was the only one who could fill the void.

Emptiness is a consequence of idolatry. When empty idols are worshiped, the worshiper becomes just as vacant. Enough of something that's not there is never enough. Only when we make God the object of our worship will we then find all the things that we were searching for in our pursuit of money, love, sex, family, career, and status.

It's easy to think we'd never sell our bodies like a prostitute and so we dismiss Gomer as someone beneath us, a woman without the moral values that elevate us above her. But if you look up the definition of "prostitution" in the dictionary, you'll discover that the secondary meaning goes beyond sexual commerce and refers to any instance of selling your talents for an unworthy cause. If we're honest, we engage in this kind of prostitution every day with the idols we hold on to. We sell ourselves short and give our talents to undeserving causes.

Similarly, Gomer gave herself to unworthy goals for the unfulfilled needs in her life. Maybe it was to enjoy the thrill of the chase or to feel desirable, to be pursued and wanted, the sense of false intimacy that seemed to be within her control. There was likely a sense of power she experienced, both over the men she encountered as well as her husband. But gradually, eventually, all these unworthy goals just left her more unfulfilled.

I think it's sort of like eating potato chips. Remember the old Lay's commercial, "Bet you can't eat just one"? Think about your favorite kind of chip or snack for a moment. It's hard to stop yourself from having just one, and the next thing you know, the bag's empty, but your stomach isn't much fuller. You can load up on carbs and an hour later you're hungry again—they just don't last. The more you eat, the more you want.

FORGET YOU

In the book of Hosea, we read some powerful passages on how people chased after counterfeit gods. God says of Israel: "She doesn't realize it was I who gave her everything she has—the grain, the new wine, the olive oil; I even gave her silver and gold. But she gave all my gifts to Baal" (2:8). Known as the "storm god," Baal was worshiped in the ancient cultures around Israel. He was thought to bring rain and fertility to the land, which produced abundant crops. God provided for His people their food and wine, which they then sacrificed on an altar of another god! Imagine your spouse giving you a beautiful piece of jewelry to commemorate his love for you, which you then take and use to entice a hookup at your neighborhood bar. It seems shockingly unbelievable when we look at it this way, but how much more inconceivable—and painful—it must have been for God.

In one of the most tragic verses in the Bible, God says, "She put on her earrings and jewels and went out to look for her lovers but *forgot all about me*" (Hosea 2:13).

How is it possible to forget someone who loves you so deeply and passionately?

Easier than you might think. Just before heading out the door to make a recent ice cream run, I asked Lori what kind she preferred. She thought for a second and said, "Get anything—as long as it doesn't have bananas or nuts."

Easy enough, I thought, and jumped in my car. Fifteen minutes later, I'm staring at the dozens of gallons and countless flavors in the upright freezer at the store, frantically trying to remember what she said. Did she say she liked bananas but not nuts? Or the other way around? Or did she want both? All I remembered was something about bananas and nuts, so I grabbed cartons of both banana split and pecan praline.

When I walked in the door and proudly displayed my selections, she looked at me flabbergasted and kindly asked, "How could you go wrong with only two options? Are you kidding me?"

Ever been there? How many items do we forget in the course of an average day? We forget our glasses, car keys, homework, report deadline, or a friend's birthday. It's so much easier than we realize to forget God.

When we forget God, it's rarely that we wake up and choose to do it. It's often subtle and slow, gradual over the course of one day after another. We get busy with work, with school and family responsibilities, even with church. The kids play sports and have music lessons. We have concerts and events and golf games and club meetings. Like the frog in the kettle of water that never realizes it's getting warmer until it's too late, we find ourselves gradually slipping away. Imperceptibly we just remove God from the place He used to have in our life.

We also have the human tendency to take things for granted. Once we have a pay raise, for example, it becomes the norm and we absorb it into our lives. We get a new car and it's exciting, but before too long there are just as many empty French fry cartons and crumbled-up Cheetos between the seats as in the old one. Many times we simply take God for granted as well. Perhaps in this sense we act more like a spoiled kid than an unfaithful spouse. God blesses us and provides for us, and we just take it all for granted and move forward in life.

When your prayers become sporadic and random, usually when you're in great need or difficulty, it often points to a shift in your heart. When you can write your name in dust on the cover of your favorite Bible, this might be a problem. When you can't remember the last time you were at church, or the last meaningful spiritual insight you learned, it could be that you're simply taking Him for granted. I'm not saying you don't care about Him. You know He's there for you. But you have so many more urgent things to do than connect with Him. Before you know it, God can say the same thing to you and me that He said to Israel, they *"forgot all about me."*

FANTASY FOOTBALL

In order to get our memory back—and more important, our relationship with God restored—we must look at who we are and how we're made. At the core of who we are as men and women, God created us to be "imagers" and "worshipers."

God made us to reflect aspects of His personhood; we're literally made in His image. Because of this, we will always tend to look like what we worship. "We become what we worship,"[2] explains Bible scholar Greg Beale. "God has made humans to reflect Him, but if they do not commit themselves to Him, they will not reflect Him but something else in creation. At the core of our beings we are imaging creatures. It is not possible to be neutral on this issue: we either reflect the Creator or something in creation."[3]

The most dangerous idols usually result from good things in our lives. This is spelled out clearly in Paul's letter to the Romans when he describes humanity as "exchanging the glory of God" and the "truth of God" for God's gifts in creation (1:23–25, NIV). Our desires, which were meant for God-fulfillment, are reduced and corrupted, leading us to form our own gods, usually tangible entities that give us more immediate gratification. Something that's meant to be enjoyed gets supersized in our search for pleasure, security, or relief from the pain of life. Before you know it, something good has eclipsed everything else in our lives—including God.

The desire for love and romance is a great thing. But if this desire becomes all-consuming and turns into a life quest for a woman or a man, it can become an idol. The desire to be pursued is one God hard-wired into women, but God is ultimately the one who can fulfill this desire. When there is a pull to constantly seek romantic fantasies through the latest Nicholas Sparks novel or Katherine Heigl rom-com movie, one can replace the fulfillment God offers for a Hollywood substitute that just creates unrealistic expectations and frustrations.

Or take sports, which I enjoy as much as the next person. I've never thought of myself as one of those fanatics you see in the end zone with their faces painted in team colors and wearing a ridiculous block of cheese, a Viking helmet, or a pirate hat. However, I recently came to the realization that perhaps there wasn't that much separating us after all.

When a friend called me and said he had a free ticket to a *Monday Night Football* game in Dallas, the Cowboys versus the Redskins, I was there! Every fan's fantasy, right? I'd watched Cowboys' games since I was old enough to sit in my dad's lap rocking in his brown lounger every Sunday afternoon. All I had to do was find a way to get to Dallas. It had been a couple of years since I'd been to a game so I was pumped. Just thinking about the fun I'd have with my friends, the experience of being with other fans, made me happier than I'd been in a while. That week I walked around with a spring in my step. I smiled a lot. The kind of smile that says, "I've got good news." It was one of those things I couldn't wait to tell people about!

And with this kind of good news inside me, there was nothing that could bring me down. I had to make some tough leadership calls at church, but I'm going to the Monday night game! My car was acting up (my speedometer read 120 mph as other cars blew past on the freeway), but I'm going to the Monday night game! My good news gave me a positive outlook because it pointed beyond the immediate. I had something special to look forward to that bad news couldn't touch.

Studying my Bible that week, I turned to the passage where Paul writes; "Above all, you must live as citizens of heaven, conducting yourselves in a manner worthy of the Good News about Christ" (Philippians 1:27). Whenever I had read this verse before, I had always been drawn to an emphasis on how living worthy of Christ means living a better life. What impacted me this time, though, was the fact that I'm called to live worthy of the *good news* of Christ. I'm called to live as someone who has good news.

It hit me like a Dallas defender sacking Washington's quarterback. I had let the fact that I was going to a *football* game shape my outlook all week more directly than the *good news of Jesus*! How much more should the good news reframe my perspective? After all, I'll forget who even won the game within a short period of time, especially if it's the other team!

AMERICAN IDOLS

My encounter with *Monday Night Football* reminded me that sports enthusiasts are even called "fans," derived from the Latin word *fanaticus,* which means "inspired by a deity, frenzied, from [the word] *fanum* [which means] temple."[4] Certainly, the immeasurable and infinite splendor of God is more thrilling than any fourth-quarter touchdown pass. But if we compared the emotion in an NFL stadium on Sunday afternoon with the fervor in a church on Sunday morning, we might be surprised.

Please don't read me wrong. I'm not trying to be a religious whacko who suggests people shouldn't appreciate life. I enjoy sports, and I had a blast at the Monday night game! I'm just surprised at how quickly some good, less obvious things, can begin to impact my outlook and heart *more* than the good news of Jesus. If these good things go unchecked and are allowed to grow in unhealthy ways, they can become something else and nudge God from first place in our hearts.

And it's not just sports or romance. Idols can be found

anywhere—in the basement or kitchen or at work. Even put-
tering in the garage or scrapbooking can become an idol when
it consumes extreme amounts of our time and pushes things
like faith to little more than an afterthought. (But I'd suggest
you work on your own life before pointing out what you see as
your spouse's idols!)

The problem with idolatry is not only that we are focusing
on something (or someone) other than God. Much of idolatry
comes back to self-preoccupation and "self-worship." Our present social media–obsessed culture is often described as "narcis-
sistic." This word comes to us thanks to Narcissus, a young man
in a Greek myth who was so good looking that he couldn't take
his eyes off himself—literally! When he looked into a pool of water and saw his reflection, he was so enamored with it that he just
sat and stared. He finally starved himself to death because he refused to take his gaze off his own handsome reflection.

How do we know if we're engaging in this kind of self-focus to
the point that it clouds our God-focus? How do we know if we're
becoming too preoccupied with ourselves and nudging God out
of first place? These are tough questions. When we regularly react to criticism with rage, shame, or the tendency to humiliate
the person criticizing, we should ask why. When we take advantage of other people to achieve our own goals, it points to
what's going on in our hearts. When we have excessive feelings
of self-importance, exaggerate our achievements and talents, and
become preoccupied with fantasies of success, power, or ideal
love, these are red flags. When we Google ourselves all the time
and obsess about the number of friends or followers we have in
our social media presence, it can be a symptom of a greater issue.
Usually, we are making it about us when we have unreasonable

expectations of favorable treatment (also known as entitlement), need constant attention and admiration, and disregard the feelings of others. Pursuing our own selfish goals, we begin to lose the ability to feel compassion for others.

In our culture we're encouraged to lean into these behaviors because we spend a lot of time trying to ensure that others notice us. We wear the right clothes, live in the cool neighborhood, drive the latest hybrid sports car, and name-drop online. We work hard to create a successful brand for ourselves, to be important, successful, attractive, chic, and glamorous.

However, God challenges us to realize we were not created to be made much of, but to make much of Him. At our core, we're not created for fame. We're made to make God famous, designed to love Him with all of our heart, without leaving room for would-be idols. And until we realize God rescued us for His fame and not our own, we'll miss the ultimate purpose for life, which is Him.

We are found when we realize our center is outside ourselves and our achievements, in God Himself. David Powlison explains, "God never accepts me 'as I am.' He accepts me 'as I am in Jesus Christ.' The center of gravity is different. The good news does not allow God's love to be sucked into the vortex of our lust for acceptability and worth in and of itself. Rather it radically decenters people—what the Bible calls 'fear of the Lord' and 'faith'—to look outside themselves."[5] Turning to God and looking beyond ourselves puts us on a pathway to more pleasure, not less! In God's presence is endless pleasure. Where idols ultimately kill pleasure, God fulfills it.

Gomer didn't seem to comprehend this any better than we do. Hosea offered her stability, security, and love that would have met many of the core needs in her life. But again and again, she took a shortcut to that fulfillment and continued the cycle of unfaithfulness. She substituted sex for genuine love. She exchanged the cheap thrill of being desired by a stranger for the substantive joy of being known and appreciated inside and out by someone committed to her.

She traded the foundation of security that comes in facing one's past, making restitution, and receiving forgiveness for the vehement denial that comes from someone blinded by their own sin. Gomer just kept slamming the door on her past, and on her painful emotions, by living completely in the adrenaline-fueled chaos of the now. Too often, I'm afraid we make similar substitutions.

THE REAL THING

It's become pretty common to find substitutes in every area of our life today. Living in Vegas, I can go to the strip and think I'm in Paris, Venice, or New York just based on the landmarks and opulent décor of a variety of casinos, all of which are nice substitutes for the real places. If I go to Costco and they're out of the sale item I want, they'll give me a substitute for the same price. For seafood lovers, there's even crab-tastic premium *imitation* crab. (Now, that's scary!)

While substitutes are sometimes necessary and acceptable, spiritual alternatives never satisfy. If we want to experience the abundant life Jesus told us He came to bring, then we must accept no substitutes. We're called to return our hearts to the One who loves us like no other, our creator—God.

So how do we stay focused on the real thing? One practice I've found helpful in dethroning idols is a gut check. Now I'm not talking about looking in a full-length mirror and sucking in your midsection, but rather pausing to see where your heart is on a regular basis. I'm talking about the kind of gut check in which you stop and consider your motives, purpose, and ambitions. The kind of self-assessment that reveals what you're chasing and why.

I recently lost one of the greatest men I have ever known in my life, my father. He was from a family that didn't have much, from the other side of the tracks, as he would say. Dropping out of high school to serve in World War 2, he lied about his age to enlist just as many of his friends did. He fought in the Battle of the Bulge and in Germany as a master sergeant in the Army and a tank commander. He committed his life to Jesus and found Him faithful even in the horror of war. He went on to become a small business owner and a remarkable man of character.

In the hospital before he passed away, he was in a lot of pain, in and out of awareness. He would look up and say, "Well, it's about time we wrap this up." I knew what he was getting at. At one point he kept being shocked by his heart defibrillator, and he mistakenly thought it was what was keeping him alive. He sat up after getting zapped and said, "You get that heart doctor in here now to turn this thing off. I paid him a lot of money and I should be dead by now!" (Yep, that's my dad.)

The last time I talked to him, I went in and held his hand, and he looked at my sister and me, smiled, and said, "You're good kids. I love you. I'll see you on the other side. I'm going for a walk in the sunshine." Through tears I told him how much he meant to me. I shared that I loved him deeply and agreed I'd see him soon. I thanked him for being an awesome father and man of God, and I committed to him that I'd try to follow in his footsteps as a dad and a man. He closed his eyes and that was the last time we ever spoke. A few days later, he passed peacefully at hospice.

Losing my father brought a lot of things back into perspective for me. It caused me to reflect on my life and do a major gut check. Seeing him at the end of his life reminded me that when I get to the same place in my own life, nobody will care about attendance numbers at the church I led or how many books I've sold or interviews I've done. Nobody will care about so much of what I can get caught up in with life.

What really matters on your deathbed? Your relationship with God and others; it's a short list.

A gut check grounds you and helps you zero in on what may be coming before God in your life. Certainly a loss or crisis has a way of forcing you to consider what is most important. Yet you don't have to wait for something like this; you can reflect and pause and consider what's coming between you and God each day. On the other side of this reflection is a return to God's fulfillment.

CELEBRATE GOOD NEWS

Another way we can focus on the real thing is to celebrate the good news of Jesus daily. Think about what you're really looking forward to in the next month—a birthday, a family gathering, a concert by your favorite band, even a *Monday Night Football* game! Does the kind of joy you experience in your anticipation of this event seem stronger than the joy you experience from encountering God on a daily basis? The point of the question isn't to take you away from things you like to do in your life. Enjoy the game! But ask the question because it helps pin down an often-wayward heart.

And undoubtedly it's not only the things that excite us in life that can try and replace God. A friend of mine, a theological professor and all-around incredible person, went through a period of depression that lingered in his life. It came to a point where he kept a loaded gun in his office drawer and daily flirted with the impulse to end his own life.

One weekend taking communion at church, he had a life-changing experience. He was praying through his list of sins, as he did every time he took communion, and suddenly he just stopped and said, "God, I'm sorry, not just because of what I have done, but because I have broken relationship with you." The tears flowed as it all came out in a torrent.

God had become status quo—reduced to attend church, read your Bible, pray through the list of sins. The rules had become anchors around his neck and they were pulling him under. No matter how hard he tried, he couldn't keep it all together. He was taking himself way too seriously and not taking the grace of God seriously enough. The day it all began to change was at rock bottom when he came back to that simple relationship with God.

The weeks after this moment, he seemed to completely change before my eyes. He smiled again, even started cutting up and acting ornery. This kid inside him that had been buried under his performance was freed as he based his life again on the foundation of God's love and mercy. He just came back to the fact that God pursued him in his sin, found him, saved him, redeemed him, and is still pursuing him each day. He was free to live as an imperfect person who is perfectly loved.

Perhaps it's time to look beyond your frustrations, fatigue, and list of sins and see again the God who continues to pursue you. He's not sitting back with His arms crossed waiting to see if you can pull it together. He's not trying to convert you so you can just go to church, be good, and make your mama happy. Jesus didn't die so you could only perform your religious duties. He died so you can be in a divine romance with a living God. Out of that union everything flows. He's more concerned about *you* than all the sacrifices, energy, and time you've committed to Him.

This good news of Christ should point you forward and soften the bad news of life. The dishwasher breaks, but you have good news! Your back aches, but you have good news! The pipes leak, but you have good news! You get a flat tire the afternoon your cell phone battery dies, but you have good news! You've been let in on a remarkable mystery—the God of the universe loves you and accepts you in Christ. He delights in you and you in Him. This should shape you and bring you joy. So I've been looking at my life and asking, *"Am I acting like a person whose life is shaped by the good news of Christ?"*

ENJOYING GOD

We can also stay focused on the real thing by seeking to intentionally enjoy God. Have you ever wondered what really brings God pleasure? It is no secret. The Bible tells us plainly what we can do that delights Him. God's "delight is in those who fear him, those who put their hope in his unfailing love" (Psalm 147:11).

When you trust Him with your daily needs and your deepest longings, when you believe His love will not fail you, He delights. He commits to rejoicing in you with all His heart and soul and doing good to you. What a beautiful eye-opener! Your trust in God's faithful love is something He exalts in! When you pray, you bring God pleasure. He "delights in the prayers of the upright" (Proverbs 15:8). Prayer acknowledges your dependence on God and your commitment to Him. When you obey, you bring God pleasure (1 Samuel 15:22). Since God delights in giving you mercy, you can cheerfully obey from the refuge of His love. Each day you can not only enjoy God, but also bring Him joy!

Everything we give our ultimate allegiance to that is smaller than God will simply fail us. The hunger for meaning, the desire for pleasure, the thirst for love or romance that draws us to so many things can only be fulfilled in God. I see this every day on the streets of Las Vegas. The self-proclaimed "Sin City" has established its reputation. But the untold story is the brokenness, the pain, and the hurt of its inhabitants—the inevitable result of a city designed to max out your senses and push your pleasures to the limit.

When people come to church in Vegas, they don't need to be convinced there is sin or darkness. They've lived it, seen it, and tasted it. They know that the idols of sex, pleasure, and entertainment are empty in themselves. They come seeking God, seeking substance, and seeking something that will last beyond a momentary flash. They often don't feel they can ever be forgiven for things they have done or things they have seen, but what they find is a God who not only takes them back, but has been pursuing them all along.

They discover that God's love and grace are bigger than anything they imagined. It's much more than a religion; they have entered a relationship with a loving and grace-filled God. He never gave up on them. Just as He's never given up on you. And by keeping this divine romance first in our hearts, we experience the joy for which we were created.

So far our guy Hosea is off to a really rough start. His wife is cheating on him and his kids have horrible names and it's all very *intense*. We're a long way from Mayberry. No wonder this story has never been made into a movie! This intensity captures God's divine obsession for us and calls us back to Him, but we can miss the big picture and get the wrong message.

Maybe you're already feeling pressure. Frustrated by your wayward heart, all this passion of God may feel overwhelming. You know you need to deal with your sin and idolatry, but what do you do when you fall back into the same destructive habits *again* and *again*? You sense the pull to gear up and try harder, to run fast after God, but you've got a hunch that, within a month, your sprint will go through a slow fade into a weary limp.

More guilt and condemnation are not really what God is trying to get at by calling our attention to idolatry. God's pursuit, not ours, is primary over each page in Hosea, and His intensity only puts an exclamation point on His love. If He cares this much, rejoice with certainty that He'll meet you in your sin, love you in your betrayal, and give you strength when you're limping along. How could He not nurture you with His mighty arms? How could He not fan into flame even the smallest ember in your heart toward Him? How could He not be faithful to you even in your fatigue?

If it seems too good to be true, just wait, it gets better! We'll turn our attention now to this miracle of God's grace that leads Him to pursue us to begin with, even as we wrestle with our sin and idolatry. Even when in our weariness we don't wrestle at all. We'll be inspired by Hosea to accept God's grace in the deeper places of our hearts and stop the brutal cycles of shame, guilt, and performance before God.

PART TWO

→

pursued in grace

CHAPTER FOUR

→

bad romance

Grace is given to heal the spiritually sick, not
to decorate spiritual heroes.

—*Martin Luther*

one of my favorite unexpected moments as a pastor in Las
Vegas happened at a concert by the Irish rock band U2. Las Vegas's MGM Grand Garden Arena was sold out for back-to-back
shows, and twenty thousand people packed in from everywhere,
giving me a distinct sense of claustrophobia. We endured a bad
Reggae opening act, but once the dark-haired, sunglasses-wear-
ing Bono took the stage with the band, I forgot all about the
crowd and just enjoyed the music and my friends. The great thing
about U2 is they have had so many hit songs everybody knows
the words so their shows feel like massive sing-alongs.

What blew me away was a moment that I knew was coming.
In hundreds of shows, Bono sings the spiritual "Amazing Grace."
This night was no different, and suddenly the MGM Grand felt
like a church with thousands of voices singing, "Amazing Grace,

how sweet the sound, thàt saved a wretch like me." They have
done this all over the world, but nothing prepared me for the
volume or the beauty of it live. Here were thousands of people,
many of whom would never darken the door of a church, and
they were singing so *loudly*. The guy next to me had his hands
in the air and his eyes closed. Clearly this was more than just
a karaoke moment for him. I stood there and looked at everyone—this was *my city* belting out "Amazing Grace," this was Sin
City but people sang like it was God's City. The experience just
floored me. I prayed that God would make the words to the song
true in all of our lives.

"Amazing Grace" is one of the most recognized songs in the
English language. So what keeps most of us from experiencing
the same kind of revolution described so well in the song? Or
to ask this question a radically different way: Why would any
woman repeatedly leave her loving husband and the security of
their home to go sell her body to strangers on the streets? Why
would Gomer repeatedly violate her marriage vows to a man
who must love her (if he didn't love her, Hosea could divorce her
with cause under the Jewish law)? Why settle for bad romance
when she could have true love?

Bottom line, I believe it's because we don't really grasp
grace, precisely when we assume we do. We can't fathom the
sheer irrational motivation of divine love. His grace is so amazing that we tend to doubt it, no matter how often we hear
about it.

We've seen that God is willing to go to extreme lengths to foster our connection with Him. Like a jealous lover, He wants to
be first in our lives. He's not pursuing us fundamentally in anger
or hate. He's pulling us over to show us how to really enjoy the

ride! This life-giving relationship with God can lead us past our weariness and shake us out of our indifference.

No matter how much you've heard about God's grace, there are more depths to explore. Ultimately, it is grace more than anything else that can renovate our spiritual journey and move us past the "It's Complicated" status with God. Anyone who is tired of learning about God's grace doesn't value it completely. When we finally get what grace is all about, it's like a song that you listen to hundreds of times and appreciate more every time you hear it.

Over the next several chapters, we'll look at what makes God's grace truly astonishing and consider how we miss it in our lives. With the story line of Hosea as our guide, we'll see what God's grace delivers us *from* and, more important, what His grace rescues us *to*. We'll consider the negative impact of guilt and shame and the price that was paid to free us from their grip. The need to perform for God is always a temptation, so we'll think about what it means to rest in Him. Both Gomer and Hosea find grace marvelous again as they overcome certain barriers. We'll explore our own obstacles to God and broaden our experience of Him.

GRACE JOB

One of our obstacles with God is we all too quickly assume we grasp grace. We may think, "God forgives, right? It's like His job. He loves me through my failures, as do my parents, I get it. We're clear." Yet when God's grace becomes too familiar, it ceases being His grace at all.

To get the fullness of God's love way down deep in our bones, we must play the grace song again. We must reconsider how we are applying it in our lives and what difference it makes. Grace is miraculous and wonderful and irrational and more than a little nuts, and therefore usually beyond our ability to fully comprehend. It defies our categories and blows up our conception of how relationships work. Only in understanding we'll never fully grasp the depth of God's grace can we open ourselves up to new levels of amazement and wonder as we experience it.

The fact that many believers have been scandalized by Hosea's story line over the centuries and have buried it in history just shows our tendency to reduce grace to our categories. Religion is often threatened by radical grace. We turn grace into whatever we think is acceptable, which often means whatever is moral and decent. But there is little about God's wild grace that fits into the category of social acceptability. This is way beyond the love of a sentimental romance movie.

The more we grow in grace, the less inclined we are to give ourselves to alternates for God. So set aside any preconceived notions that you've somehow moved beyond grace or that grace is elementary. Don't check out because you've heard the "God forgives us" stuff many times before. You may find, as I have, that nothing grounds us, nothing sustains us, nothing keeps us going like God's grace.

In fact, when we don't fully lean into grace, we find ourselves stuck in repeating the same old patterns. We hit roadblocks. We crash into walls. We end up on detours that lead us right back to the idols we tried to leave in the first place. We settle for a few moments of temporary comfort instead of the eternal security that God offers us.

OBSTACLE COURSE

Gomer must have known what this vicious cycle of seemingly endless repetition felt like. If she made an effort to leave this life behind and embrace a new life with Hosea, then surely these detours to receiving grace and forgiveness led her back into the old stuff, into the old spiral of shame and regret. She, like each of us, had to recognize the emotional, relational, and spiritual barriers blocking her path back to the one waiting to love and forgive her completely. Let's consider some obstacles that kept her from fully seizing God's grace.

Gomer would have faced emotional barriers to receiving Hosea's love and forgiveness, including complex layers of shame, guilt, fear, anger, and grief. According to Annie Lobert, whose story I shared with you earlier, approximately 69 percent of the women getting out of the sex industry have post-traumatic stress syndrome (PTSD). These symptoms include things like an inability to sleep, anxiety and depression, emotional numbness, flashbacks, and a hyper sense of alertness. Often these ladies exhibit emotional challenges similar to those of combat veterans returning from war.

Many of these women maintain emotional ties to their pimps because, as strange as it may seem, they love them. This tends to blind them to how unhealthy this type of love is so they consistently return to him no matter how abusive he may be. On average, these girls have a propensity to go back *five to seven times* to their old lifestyle before they completely walk away. We see Gomer trapped in this same kind of pattern, returning to her old ways again and again, even in the midst of Hosea's constant love.

Okay, so my guess is many of us don't have an abusive pimp

we return to repeatedly, but nonetheless, this cycle illustrates our own journey with God. We prostitute our talents, our identities, our truest selves for unworthy causes. When we come to our senses, the emotional barrier to fully receiving love is enormous. We don't think we are worth God's love. We feel hopeless, afraid it's too late to ever be any more than what we've become.

Gomer would surely have wrestled with all this and may have felt she deserved to be treated in an abusive manner. The very love Hosea showed her, the kindness and tenderness, could have felt as an affirmation of how unworthy she was. It could have been the very thing pushing her away.

The bottom line is that Gomer, like so many of us, couldn't love herself and therefore believed that no one else could love her.

Layers of painful emotions aren't the only obstacles to embracing grace. Years of living far from God make for plenty of relational challenges as well. We get distorted perspectives of what it means to give and receive love to other people—and ourselves. In Gomer's case, she faced that challenge by disassociating herself from the act of earning love by giving her customers what they wanted. If she was ever to be in a healthy marriage, she would have a lot of past rubble to work through, and it would take a special man and a special kind of love to heal her.

Finally, we must overcome our spiritual baggage about how we view God and how He views us if we are ever going to live in the fullness of His grace. Too often we cling to false views that allow us to feel like victims or to feel justified in our idolatry. We blame God for the hardships in our life, including our habits and idols.

I recently saw a guy with a tattoo that said, GOD HATES US

ALL. For some people, this is easy to believe. We often hate certain things about ourselves and we despise our past mistakes and screwups. It is easy—and sometimes convenient—just to believe that God sees the worst and it stops there.

Gomer must have wrestled with this kind of barrier with Hosea and with God. There would be extreme self-hate for what she had done. It would have taken a lot to overcome the feelings that God was just angry with her all the time. A powerful love was needed to scrub the false belief about God she had tattooed on her heart.

However, the great news of the gospel is a radical cleansing agent. It reminds us we are in a more horrible, filthy state than we could ever imagine because of our sin, but that God loves us more radically than we can ever possibly grasp. What brings the gospel into proper weight is both sides, the reality of human sin, but also the extreme grace of God.

There is a lot of talk about grace in Christian teaching and publications, and yet what is surprising is that studies show most Americans miss grace completely. Most people seem to continue believing that knowing God is all about morality. Surveys by social scientists as well as religious institutions consistently indicate the vast majority of adults in the United States actually believe that a connection with God is about right behavior; it is about earning your way to God's favor (or at least His tolerance) by living a good, moral life.

It's worth mentioning a study by highly respected Notre Dame sociologist Christian Smith. He did an extensive study on teen spirituality in America and found the view of God among young people in America who are Christians does not include a reliance on God's grace. Studies show that these are the same views of their parents. Smith's conclusion about American beliefs are summed up well by Michael Horton:[1]

1. God created the world.
2. God wants people to be good, nice, and fair to each other, as taught in the Bible and most world religions.
3. The central goal of life is to be happy and to feel good about oneself.
4. God does not need to be particularly involved in one's life except when needed to resolve a problem.
5. Good people go to heaven when they die.

Smith called this predominant view "Moralistic Therapeutic Deism." It's moralistic in that adherents believe it's all about being good to get right with God. It's therapeutic since it's about how to solve life's problems in order to be happy. And it's deistic because they assume God created the world and then stepped away to let it run its course.

Smith concluded that for Americans: "Being religious is about being good and it's not about forgiveness....It's unbelievable the proportion of conservative Protestant teens who do not seem to grasp the elementary concepts of the gospel concerning grace....It's across all traditions."[2]

Without a framework for grace, we are left with religion and morality in a vacuum. Everything is boiled down to checklists of right and wrong, and we are tempted to become smug, feeling superior in our "goodness." We start to think we are better, we are "together," we have it figured out. We aren't like "those" people.

In our arrogance, we merely substitute our own pious actions over God's. If we believe or *act as if* a person gets to heaven because they live good lives, then we still don't fully understand the message of grace. Grace means the *undeserved* favor of God. Grace communicates that no matter how good or bad you have been, you'll never be good enough. Jesus lived and died in your place and your salvation is not about your own acts of goodness, but about God's mercy and forgiveness.

We're all sinners who desperately need grace every day. As we are continually amazed by grace, we become less interested in one-upping each other on the "good" scale but in living before God with gratefulness and generosity because of His goodness to us. We gladly face the many barriers that separate us from experiencing grace and move through them. Only then can we come alive in the fullness of His joy and the purpose for which He created us.

HONEYMOON IN VEGAS

Maybe part of the problem is that we try to wrap our minds around the concept of grace when it's our hearts we should focus on. We may believe in grace to some degree, but do we live like it? Grace will always be outlandish, wild, unpredictable, undeserved. Based on human logic, or even on the way most people would feel, God's grace is certifiably crazy or it is not grace.

What would compel a husband to keep bringing his wife home from the bed of strangers? How did he not lose hope and just give up? Through all of Gomer's unfaithfulness, Hosea remained faithful in his love and grace, just as God is faithful. In fact, his response seems the opposite to what most of us would be inclined to do.

What do you do when someone has cheated on you, lied to you, deceived you, and done it all defiantly and shamelessly? Now that's a bad romance! No one would fault us if we said, "Enough is enough—I'm done!" But that's not the response we see from Hosea—or from God. He knows His people will eventually face the harsh reality that what they're chasing doesn't satisfy them. He says of His people that: "When she runs after her lovers, she won't be able to catch them. She will search for them but not find them. Then she will think, 'I might as well return to my husband, for I was better off with him than I am now'" (Hosea 2:7).

But it's not enough for His people to return to Him by default. He wants our hearts. He wants all of us. God says, "Therefore, I'm going to allure her" (Hosea 2:14 NIV). The word "allure" in the original language is a romantic term. God is going to romance His people and woo them back. He's literally going to charm them.

Talk about not making sense! The people of Israel just had a spiritual affair on God. They turned their backs on Him, forgot about Him, denied Him, and worshiped other gods. Yet God wants to allure them! He will "lead her into the desert and speak tenderly to her there" (Hosea 2:14). It's no accident He wants to lead them back to the desert; it had been a sacred place for the Israelites when He delivered them out of captivity in Egypt. As harsh as a desert can be, this was the place where they first experienced God in this new, intimate, relational way.

For forty years they roamed in the desert and learned God was holy, good, true, and just. They learned to trust Him. To rely on Him for food, water, guidance, and direction. Now, metaphorically speaking, God wanted to take them back to the desert for a second honeymoon. There they are going to learn again He's their God, that He will never turn His back on them. He remains faithful even though they became faithless.

ROMANCING THE STONE

God continues to allure you and me the same way. Even when our hearts feel like stone, He's committed to romancing us until we come back home spiritually. His grace softens our hearts, impacts our will, allows us to heal, and empowers us to face the pressures of life. As I grow in grace, it expands my whole perspective of God and of life. My heart overflows with the sheer surprise of being loved and accepted as I am in Christ. I am free to love others as someone who isn't perfect and doesn't expect others to be perfect. I can accept people as they are: flawed, imperfect, selfish, hurting, broken, daring-to-hope people.

I'm still amazed by this thing called grace. It never gets old. And I guess it's probably because, as I mature, I realize how badly I need it on so many different levels in my life. I've noticed the further I get from my awareness and dependence on God's grace, the higher the discouragement levels rise in my life. Everything looks more discouraging apart from grace.

Without a mindfulness of grace, the memory of past mistakes and old sins can still haunt me. Current difficulties can overpower me because I can't see how I can manage them on my own. I start comparing myself to other people and become demoralized because I don't have their talents or abilities. And people and their problems can overwhelm me.

Drifting from God's grace, we depend more and more on ourselves. The truth is none of us can do it by ourselves and *we're not supposed to.* Countless of us have tried to make a break with any number of sins based on their own power. We read the "self-help" books and take a "do-it-yourself" attitude, an attitude that can become one of the biggest stumbling blocks to true intimacy with God. The shortcoming of self-help is that we need *more than ourselves* and *more than our help;* we need spiritual healing. We rarely think in terms of spiritual healing. We go to a book or a friend for help, but without the spiritual dimension, we find it falls short again and again. So we go out and buy another self-help book! God invites us into a deeper healing accomplished by His grace.

I was challenged in this area of my life when I went in for some counseling. I wanted to talk through some things and seek to remain relatively emotionally healthy. (I did say "relatively"!) My counselor listened to me share about my life and history. He was asking question after question, but he was listening intently.

After he heard me talk for a while, he said, "Jud, let me repeat back to you a phrase you used, because I think there is something there we need to consider. As you were speaking about your life, you used this phrase more than once—'do it on my own with God.'" The reason that is important is we have a kind of logic we develop in our hearts about God and our life. Often this way of thinking comes from our past or our upbringing or our church experience, but it may not come from God.

He continued, "What concerns me is that your emphasis seems be on the words 'on my own.'" Now my first thought was, "I didn't say that and why exactly did I come to this counselor?" But I had said it and he patiently showed me my own self-deception. I had said things like, "College was hard, but I did it on my own with God and graduated at the top of my class." Or, "Being a pastor is incredibly challenging, but I've learned to do it on my own with God." I even said, "Staying clean from drugs for over twenty-three years is something I'm proud of. I did it on my own with God." Are you *kidding* me? Writing these words is hard because I see how ridiculous they sound. I did none of this on my own. Everything I've accomplished in life has been a gift. I had God's grace not only in my own life, but through great people around me who helped me along. All of this revealed that while I talked a lot about grace, the truth was that I had a long way to grow in this area. I had developed some absurd logic that showed I believed I relied primarily on myself *precisely when I didn't*. I still wasn't applying God's grace after all these years, sermons, Bible studies, and books. I still needed to develop in grace. Thankfully, God's grace applies to every challenge, every obstacle, and every decision, even those we attribute to ourselves.

The big lesson I'm learning is I need to invite God in more and *live* from His grace. I need to stop worrying and doing it on my own, throwing "with God" in as a nice religious tagline. I need to stop idolizing my own independence and start allowing God's grace to work through me in all I accomplish. I need to stop assuming I have grace all wrapped up nicely with a bow on top when I'm not applying the depth of the gift. I need His undeserved favor far more than I ever imagined.

Thankfully, there are some things only God can do. No matter how hard we try, we simply cannot do them in our own power. This is especially true with overcoming our barriers to grace that we can't even see, much less the ones we can. God says, "I will remove the names of Baal from her lips" (Hosea 2:17).

God can remove from our lips the praise of what comes before

Him. He can remove us from destruction, from self-centeredness and self-reliance, from the paralyzing fear our idols lead us into. This is a work God must accomplish. No amount of "self-help" will work with us or with Israel. God is our only hope.

If you are tired of trying and failing in your journey with Jesus, maybe it's because you're relying on your own strength and not on God's. He can rescue you from the prison your idols have created in your pursuit of them. He can heal you from the past disappointments. He can shake you up out of apathy and indifference. If you're *trying* to keep it together, *trying* to work out your stuff, *trying* to stay involved at church, *trying* to pray more, *trying* to keep juggling everything to keep it from all crashing down, maybe you should just stop trying so much and focus again on all that God's grace covers.

Every day I wake up, I seem to do one of three things: I run at the day like a type A achiever but forget God, I run from the day and ignore or avoid God and my challenges, or I run to God and place myself under His grace not for salvation, but for becoming the person He desires. I have to make this choice every morning and it determines if my day is lived to the fullest in a big way.

I'm living under grace when I start my day with gratitude for all Jesus has done for me. When I remember the security I already have in God's love. When I push back on feeling overwhelmed or anxious by bringing my challenges to God in prayer. When I remember God's mercy to me as I view people and their problems. When I smile at the simple fact that no matter how bad or crazy the day gets, and no matter how much I stumble, I'm perfectly loved by a perfect God.

His grace is something you don't have to fully fathom to experience. And the danger often lies in quickly assuming you do understand it. It's not too late to surrender all the barriers, all the layers of junk, and be surprised. Play the grace song again! It can lead you beyond the bad romance you may have settled for up to new levels of divine love. You won't hear it a lot in our culture, but maybe the best thing you can do right now, if you're just exhausted trying to face whatever your facing, is to give up just like you did when you first came to faith. Quit. Concede. Stop running and turn yourself in. Just admit you're so tired of trying and none of it is working. This won't be news to God! He's been patiently waiting for this moment. When you give up, you make room for God to step up! Give it over to Him and take the risk of trusting Him with it. You don't need to *do it on your own* anymore.

CHAPTER FIVE

loved from death to life

Remember that his name is ultimately Love,
that he has loved us with an everlasting love
and knowing him thus, we can appropriate
unto ourselves all the gracious promises.

—*Martyn Lloyd-Jones*

the flushing stage—most kids go through it. It's way too exciting to drop a toy in the toilet and watch it swirl away. In our family, this stage went on for far too long. My son seemed overjoyed when the toilet got clogged up and I'd have to take it apart. I spent hundreds of dollars in plumbing fees to fish unbelievable things out of our toilet, some of which defied the laws of physics. Like when he flushed his sister's entire full-size Barbie doll or her pink sunglasses. That takes special hand-eye coordination to accomplish!

Once I peeked around the corner and saw him standing in the bathroom looking at the toilet. At three years old with his red-and-white Mario Brothers pajamas on, he was thinking through his options. He knew it was wrong, and if he did it, he'd be in trouble and have to sit in time-out. But there he was eyeing it. Processing. I knew exactly what was happening because he has my DNA. He was asking himself: Is it worth it anyway?

That day it wasn't worth it, but a few days later he flushed a purple toy hammer that clogged everything up. When I realized what happened, I was not in a good place. Angry and upset, I tried the count-to-ten method of parental patience management, and it just got worse by the time I hit ten. The inner pastor in me was not welling up.

I looked all over the house and couldn't find him. Then I returned to the scene of the crime and found him hiding in the bathtub behind the shower curtain. As soon as I pulled the shower curtain back, he said, "I'm sorry, Daddy."

I thought, "Yeah, I have your sorry right here, buddy!" Actually, I went easy on him. I put him in time-out and he had a few tears. Of course, about four days later he was at it again, standing in front of the toilet with a Beanie Baby in his hand, contemplating: to flush or not to flush?

ROYAL FLUSH

It's a classic study of human nature. We all have things in our lives that we know we shouldn't do, things we're drawn to or things we are tempted by. Sometimes, just like my son in front of the toilet that day, we stand before whatever that thing may be and we weigh it out in our mind. If we do it, our family or our future or our health could be in jeopardy—and if we've been doing it for a while repeatedly, we could lose everything. Yet we do it anyway. Then we hide. We don't climb in the bathtub and pull the shower curtain around us, but we hide spiritually in our lives from God.

We stick with our idols and resist God's efforts to woo us back. We think He's walked away and left us to suffer alone. Or we run and hide and wish He'd leave us alone—pretending we don't need Him and He only wants to ruin our lives and spoil our fun. But the story of Hosea and Gomer shows us otherwise.

As we saw in the last chapter, we don't have to run and hide because His grace welcomes us back. We don't have to do it on our own anymore or settle for frustration. He's inviting us into a beautiful marriage with a fairy-tale ending. We considered some of the barriers to grace that we, along with Gomer, face. Now let's reflect on the man Hosea. The more we appreciate the character of God represented in Hosea's life, the better we'll understand why those barriers to grace in our lives should not prevent us from growing in God's love.

CEREAL KILLERS

Things are looking pretty bleak in Hosea's life by Chapter 3. It's gone downhill to the point where Gomer has left once again to pursue other lovers. Hosea is alone and not sure what to do.

How many nights did he pace the floor wondering where she was? Did he sit by the door, staring at it for hours, waiting to see if she'd walk through at all, bizarrely hoping she would and she wouldn't? Did he argue with himself out loud about his love for her? His hate toward what she was doing? His jealousy toward those she gave herself to? Did he have mental movies of her in bed with other men that he couldn't shut off? Did he compare himself to those men all the time? Did he find himself repairing the wall where he'd punched a hole the night before in his watchful misery? Did he just feel like he was losing his mind?

We can assume from God's own response in Hosea that this was a horrendous season filled with unpredictable emotional highs and lows. The nights were excruciating and the days exhausting. And the waiting—would it ever end?

Finally, after all the anxious moments and struggles as a single dad of kids who must have felt abandoned, God comes to Hosea and says: "Go, show your love to your wife again, though she is loved by another and is an adulteress. Love her as the LORD loves the Israelites, though they turn to other gods and love the sacred raisin cakes" (Hosea 3:1 NIV). Sacred raisin cakes were not a new kosher cereal bar on the market. They were special cakes the Israelites ate at festivals honoring the storm god, Baal. They were worshiping another god, having their cake and eating it, too.

If the people of Israel reveled in their idolatry by eating special festival cakes honoring Baal, then Gomer reveled in her unfaithfulness by allowing her customers to provide food and clothing for her. She turned her back on the man who loved her and instead ran to the arms of imitators and manipulators.

So now the waiting is over, but Gomer isn't returning on her own. Hosea is the one to pursue, to go find his wife, who has been unfaithful, who has betrayed him, who is currently loved by another and currently an adulteress. He's actually going to track her, stalk her, and lure her back. He's to locate and woo her, to literally "go and love" her, because that's how God loves His people. If you're like me, you're thinking, *"Ri...ght."*

Yet this man trusted God enough to go after her again. There is nothing Gomer did to deserve the love of Hosea. Not only is she cheating on him—she's a serial cheater. It's not like she stopped all this and came shamefully back to Hosea, saying, "Will you take me back now?" No, she's a repeat offender who can't seem to stop herself if she wanted to. And Hosea is told to take her back to demonstrate how God treats us. Not an easy job that could be done just by sheer determination and blind obedience. Somehow, someway, Hosea must have truly loved this woman in ways that transcend our typical understanding of love.

In fact, the intensity of Hosea's love for Gomer is captured beautifully in an updated retelling in Francine Rivers's best-selling novel, *Redeeming Love.* Set during the California gold rush of the 1850s, the story shows how the power of love never gives up no matter how long it takes or how many obstacles get in the way. In *Redeeming Love,* Michael Hosea continues to pursue Angel (Gomer's character) through her unfaithfulness. He pleads with her throughout, "That's the life I want to give you…I want to fill your life with color and warmth. I want to fill it with light…Give me a chance."[1]

The book offers a picture of God's unyielding pursuit, hemming us in even as we try to run. His love is so different from our love for one another. We love each other if, because, and when. If someone doesn't meet the standards for our love, doesn't come through for us, doesn't love us the way we think they should, then we withdraw and our love grows cold. And our hearts can be vindictive and become hard.

God's love is in another category all by itself.

His love is completely undeserved.

God loves *in spite of.*

Why is this so hard to grasp? Not only do we miss His gracious nature, but we've also broadened the meaning of the word "love" to encompass just about anything we like or care for. We say we love Mexican food, we love Angry Birds or Scrabble, we love Hugh Jackman movies, or we love music. We throw this same word around for everything, but in the Hebrew language of the Old Testament, they had specific words for various kinds of love.

When we see the word "love" a couple of times in the first few verses of Hosea 3, it literally means "loyal love" as it refers to God's regard for us. It points to His covenant love for us that is based more in His faithfulness to Himself than to us. This kind of love is the kind used to describe a friend that comes up beside us and walks alongside us, shoulder to shoulder. It's a long-term kind of committed love, a bond that connects you for a life-time. He knows we're fickle, that we have idolatrous, adulterous hearts. Yet He's willing to walk alongside us and be our ally in the trenches of life. He's willing to do life with us if we'll let Him in. Hosea is to go and love Gomer from this reservoir of God's loyal love.

SWEPT OFF OUR FEET

As we've seen, letting God in can be complicated although there's really nothing we're required to do but believe and follow. We simply have to open our hearts and let God love us. We just have to be honest about our need and let God be who He is, our Father whose loyalty is beyond measure. Our life with God isn't about us trying harder, but about God completing the work He began.

Throughout Hosea, God shares His loyal love for people by pointing to the future with the phrase "in that day." It ultimately foreshadows the fulfillment of all God's promises when Jesus returns. The phrase links the restoration process God is starting with His people to its fulfillment later in the birth, death, and resurrection of Jesus. God's loyal love will see them through to the end.

God also reveals His loyal love to us through the power of contrasts. The first thing God does when He restores Israel is break down the confusion that existed between Him and the competing god, Baal. "'When that day comes,' says the LORD, 'you will call me "my husband" instead of "my master." O Israel, I will wipe the many names of Baal from your lips, and you will never mention them again'" (Hosea 2:16–17).

The term "husband" expresses the idea of a close and personal bond while the term "master" emphasizes the legal aspect of the relationship at that time. God is shifting His people's attention away from a merely legal affiliation to an intimate marriage. He's not taking control by force because He's stronger. He's not going to do it just to show us He can.

God's loyal love is also patient. Maybe you've had a stray dog or cat show up on your doorstep, clearly hungry, cold, and perhaps injured. They're lost and looking for a home. But when you open your door and reach down to pet them, they flinch and run away, afraid that once again they'll be hurt, trapped, or neglected. We want to invite them in and love them and make them part of our family if only they will let us.

I wonder if this is part of the dynamic between Hosea and Gomer. Hosea leans on God's loyal love to welcome her back. He charmed her and wooed her just as God does for His people, but she was so beaten down. Sin has scarred her so deeply. Her past loomed so densely around her, like a shroud of fog, that it was hard to see her present, hard to see anything. She didn't know how to receive real love.

Yes, it's hard to understand why a husband like Hosea would stick with that weak-willed wife of his. Maybe we're even thinking he's henpecked and simply too weak and codependent to break away from her. But that's not the case at all. In the end, he simply loves her too much to abandon her to her own bad choices. Sure, he could have used force on her or taken her to court or even had her imprisoned or stoned for adultery. But he *loved* her…cherished her…saw who she really was beneath those layers of doubt and shame and unbearable sorrow.

This takes a kind of strength that's greater than any superhero can muster in any romance novel. Take Romeo, Don Juan, Mr. Darcy, and Rhett Butler all rolled into one and you still can't come close to the kind of lover we see in Hosea. The kind of Lover we see in God.

In fact, the love of God is so powerful it sweeps us off our feet and makes us forget all about those counterfeit loves we once pursued. God says He's going to erase the worship of false gods from the people's midst. God wants to fulfill the emptiness inside us with a love that will cause all our idols to fall by the wayside. This is why I believe that conquering our idols and habitual sins is ultimately a matter of being swept up by His love rather than gritting our teeth and trying harder. If we give Him a chance, God allures us and woos us with loyal love by showing His enormous strength, patience, and gentleness.

God reminds us of this truth throughout the Bible's pages: "The eternal God is your refuge, and his everlasting arms are under you" (Deuteronomy 33:27). You cannot go so low, you cannot fall so far, you cannot fail so miserably, you cannot bomb out so big in your life that God's arms are no longer under you. No matter where you're tanking in life, God's still there. He's *not giving up* and He's going to use every chance He gets to remind you of what your life could be like in His loyal love.

EXTREME MEASURES

One of the main ways we see God's love depicted throughout the Bible is in the disparity of extremes in the work of His grace. These transformational pictures of God's grace help us see how crazy-stunning it really is. The incredible aspect of grace is not only that we are rescued *from* certain things, but also that we are rescued *to* things. It is not enough to be rescued *from* death, *from* being an orphan, *from* being a stranger, *from* darkness, or *from* peasantry, as the Bible portrays.

God didn't just bring us out of these desperate situations into neutral situations. He didn't simply move in our lives so we could keep trudging along. Unfortunately, this is where much of our grasp of grace tends to stop. Yet if we've only been rescued *from* these things, what do we do now? Where does grace actually lead us *to*?

Biblical grace invites us into a much fuller experience. God's pursuit includes what we're called *to*. This is what makes grace breathtaking. Let's explore these Biblical images and allow them to clear away some of the barriers to receiving God's sweeping grace and love.

From "Death" to "Life"

Have you ever sat next to a space invader on a flight, one of those people that just have no sense of where their armrest ends and yours begins? As someone who flies coach a lot, I find this frustrating when I'm trying to do things, like write this book!

On one particular sold-out flight, a guy sat down beside me in the middle seat. I'm sure I would have liked him if I knew him, but what followed him on to that flight was a bad case of mansmell. (Ladies, you know of what I speak!) I haven't smelled this kind of powerful odor since the school locker room after football practice! The poor guy in the window seat literally started coughing, but there was nowhere to escape the smell.

To make matters worse, the man proceeded to lean forward for a nap on his tray table with his arms beneath his head, exposing his armpits. I had checked my bag or I would have offered the guy some deodorant. But then I realized it wouldn't have helped the problem—it would only have attempted to cover it up. This poor guy in the seat next to me didn't need deodorant; he needed to be sprayed off with a fire hose! He needed a shower desperately, but he didn't realize it. I'm sure I've been there and I'll be there again, much to my wife's frustration!

Some people realize they need Jesus and they want to make themselves a little better, but they don't understand the gravity of the situation. They think Jesus provides a little niceness to life, a little spiritual air freshener to help things smell better, but they underestimate how bad sin stinks.

When it comes to our need for Jesus, we are in way more desperate need than my friend on the plane. In fact, the Bible says we are more like terminal patients on life support in the hospital who just died. We're literally *dead* in our trespasses and sins spiritually. Our need isn't for some nice cosmetics or a stick of deodorant. Our need is for total resuscitation, the new life Jesus came to give us. Sin stinks worse than we ever imagined, but Jesus came to deal with our sin.

This is often easier to see if you've lived in blatant rebellion in your life. A prostitute like Gomer who comes to her senses isn't going to be wishy-washy on her need for new life. Often the ones in a more dangerous place are those who feel a sense of moral superiority. Those who think, "I've never done what Gomer did; I've always been a good person."

The problem with this thinking is that it flies in the face of the Bible's teaching. "Even though we were dead because of our sins," Paul writes, "he gave us life when he raised Christ from the dead. (It is only by God's grace that you have been saved!)" (Ephesians 2:5). God isn't trying to make good people better. He isn't trying to take nice people and make them nicer or take normally pleasant people and make them smell better. He's trying to take dead people and bring them back to life!

And it's not like we are *only* rescued from death, like some zombies out of the show *The Walking Dead*. (Zombies aren't fully dead, but judging from the zombie genre, they'd probably like to be.) God brought us back from death *to* a beautiful life! We can live and love in His freedom and we'll spend the rest of our lives and eternities unpacking the miracle of this shift. This life takes on a richer meaning as we consider some of the other Biblical images we've been delivered to, such as adoption.

From "Orphan" to "Adopted"

The Bible often refers to the relational dynamic of how God's people who once were orphans are now adopted sons and daughters. We share the riches and favor of God our Father. As Paul explains,

"God decided in advance to adopt us into his own family by bringing us to himself through Jesus Christ" (Ephesians 1:5).

In our time, many people attempt to adopt very young children. Often their thinking is to get them at a young age before they have been scarred by other things or raised in other environments. In Paul's day, adoption was limited to people with means and often involved older individuals. If one was not going to have an heir, he would choose to adopt a son, rather than an infant, to become his heir.

Older children bring certain challenges in adoption because they are set in their ways, personality, and character. They carry the scars of the past, the wounds of careless words, and the weight of feeling unloved. However, Biblical adoption takes advantage of this fact to express the love of God, for God adopted us knowing who we were and how we were. Nobody adopts a child he or she doesn't want! God adopted us knowing all of our faults, failings, and weaknesses.

As His children, we don't have to scrape by to survive anymore; we trust our Father to provide and care for us. We don't have to sleep with one eye open, worried about who's after us or afraid of those who would rob us. We don't have to withdraw to protect ourselves, or overcompensate to prove our value and worth. He's there to hold us in His arms as His precious child, no longer orphans lost in the world. We are His children and citizens of His family.

From "Stranger" to "Citizen"

Have you ever taken a trip overseas or visited a place where you knew you did not fit in and were not particularly welcome? A few years ago I had an opportunity to visit Cuba legally and deliver medical supplies, encourage some pastors there, and visit their work. We arrived late at night, around midnight, and it wasn't long before I realized I wasn't in Kansas anymore—or any of the other forty-nine states, for that matter!

Driving from the airport, I glanced at a billboard along the highway and saw a picture of our U.S. president at the time with one word emblazoned below it: TERRORIST. Then as we proceeded to our hotel, I noticed every couple of blocks a guy in a white shirt would be hanging out on the corner. Our host told us the government positions these monitors all over the country, even in little remote mountain villages, and all they do is watch and report back what they see. This way nobody can assemble a few dozen people in their home and start an underground revolution the way Fidel Castro did when he took over the country.

Don't get me wrong, Cuba is incredibly gorgeous and the people we visited there were wonderful. However, knowing the history and tensions between the governments of the United States and Cuba, I always felt like I was being watched. I was keenly aware I was not a citizen of that country and didn't really belong there. After a week it had started to feel suffocating. So while I enjoyed my visit, I kissed the ground when we landed in the United States. It felt so good to be home, back in my own country.

When it comes to life, we wander aimlessly as foreigners in an alien land, strangers to God and His mercy. Gomer would spend years here as would God's people. On the run from the one who loves us like no other. But once we enter into life with Him, we become citizens of heaven. We are part of God's very own family.

As the Bible says, "So now you Gentiles are no longer strangers and foreigners. You are citizens along with all of God's holy people. You are members of God's family" (Ephesians 2:19).

Not only are we rescued from being strangers, but our citizenship has been transferred. Strangers don't have access to the same privileges as citizens. In the Roman world, citizens could vote and had certain rights to a fair trial without undue punishment. They could appeal to Caesar and be taken to Rome for trial. In a spiritual sense, we can take our case to God. We can depend on Him and fellowship with Him. We don't have to fear what other people can do to us because we can go to a higher authority. Our citizenship defines us as members of God's community. He's responsible to take care of us and watch our backs. And we can rest in His providential control. We live in two worlds, looking forward to heaven and bringing some of heaven to earth.

We live with anticipation of enjoying God even more profoundly in heaven. There we will experience the fulfillment God has pursued us for. There we will be able to kiss the ground, so to speak, and finally be home. But for believers, we aren't there yet, so we live on as strangers in our culture, but as citizens of heaven who have been rescued.

From "Darkness" to "Light"

Have you ever been to a place that's so dark and dreary it's hard to tell the difference between day and night? During the long winters, the short days can seem so gray and gloomy in places like Alaska and the Pacific Northwest that people begin to suffer. In fact, some people get so depressed because of the lack of sunlight, there's a clinical name for their condition: seasonal affective disorder, or SAD.

Scientists have found that light therapy, just simply getting some light on your body, can cause SAD to go away. Which explains what I witnessed on a recent visit to a Seattle office complex—fluorescent lamps with aluminum foil on almost every desk. We need light in our lives to live, and spiritually, God has done this for us by moving us from darkness to light.

Over and over again, the Bible uses language that we were once darkness and now God has made His light shine on and through us. Paul writes, "For once you were full of darkness, but now you have light from the Lord. So live as people of light!" (Ephesians 5:7–8).

Without God, we walk and live in darkness, and our hearts and minds have been dimmed in the shadows. Both Gomer and Hosea knew what this darkness was. Gomer experienced it at multiple levels. The darkness of self-hate, of love to be purchased, of all of life reduced to sexual transaction. Hosea battling the darkness of a fallen world filled with corruption and sin, the darkness of betrayal, and the anger, rage, and spite threatening within his own heart. Yet God loves us too much to abandon us to our darkness; by His grace we move into the bright sun of His care.

We're rescued from the darkness of sin to the light of salvation, from the darkness of hate to the light of love, from the darkness of greed to the light of contentment, from the darkness of hopelessness to the light of hope. We can experience joy, warmth, and fulfillment in God we never thought possible in the darkness. We leave the darkness to live in the light as royalty.

From "Peasantry" to "Royalty"

Millions of people around the world watch when the British royal family members have a wedding. We were awed by the pomp and circumstance when Prince William and Kate Middleton married. We watched as this young, beautiful bride went from being an everyday commoner like you and me to being Her Royal Highness The Duchess of Cambridge, wife of the future King of England. In a matter of minutes, she received a new identity, bestowed with an inheritance greater than you or I will probably ever see. Everything that belongs to the British royal family, including the history, castles, jewelry, properties, servants, fame, and money are now also Kate's.

In a similar way, this is what happens when we follow God. We go from having an inheritance of death to having an inheritance "in Christ" that is beyond anything we could have ever imagined. We are children of the King of Kings! We inherit all that is God's—spiritual blessings of forgiveness, joy, provision, contentment, and rest.

We are rich in love because God loved us and chose us from the foundation of the world to be united with Christ and to be His followers. We are rich in faith. Paul says, "And this same God who takes care of me will supply all your needs *from his glorious riches,* which have been given to us in Christ Jesus" (Philippians 4:19). He will supply all our needs *from* His glorious riches given *to* us in Christ! If someone is just above the poverty line and he or she offers to supply you from their riches, then you know it won't be much. But God's riches are endless. He's got all things in His hands, and *from* these riches he'll take care of us.

We inherit His riches freely given to us as members of His

royal family. We didn't earn them to begin with, and we don't have to fight to keep them. We live in security as ones who have been called into this unbelievable inheritance. God saved us from being orphans, dead in sin, strangers to God, lost in darkness and spiritual poverty, to a life of adoption as His children, alive in Him, citizens of heaven, people of light who live as God's royalty.

Think about these powerful pictures. The question isn't do you *feel* like this is true for you? The question is do you *believe* it is based on what the Bible says? As you accept the gift of what you've been rescued *to* in faith, you can act like a person experiencing the fullness of grace. Over time your feelings often tend to follow your actions and you start to *feel* like a person rescued to new life. So Paul says, "Awake, O sleeper, rise up from the dead, and Christ will give you light" (Ephesians 5:14). No more sleepwalking! Wake up to incredible things God's restored you to! Let your faith replace your fear and lead you into the bright and beautiful warmth of His care! He pursues you because He loves you in senseless, ridiculous ways beyond your imagination.

Hosea represents this wild pursuit as he goes on the hunt for Gomer. He sets aside pride and disgrace and stakes out the woman he's married to, for better or worse. Eventually he tracks her down, but he can't bring her home without a price being paid to the men who possess her now. To lift her sights to a new life, and to help her heal from shame and guilt, he'll have to buy her back. In a parallel way, God's grace can heal us of our shame and guilt, but it comes at an incredible cost, as we'll see.

CHAPTER SIX

→

price for a prostitute

I haven't always been a Christian. I didn't go
to religion to make me happy. I always knew a
bottle of Port would do that.

—*C. S. Lewis*

we have a bulldog named Roxy, who is an absolute mess of
a dog that we all adore. Every time a guest comes over to our
house, she gets real excited and wets the floor. She just lets herself go! Apparently, her bladder can't contain the joy. So we're
always cleaning up after Roxy.

She snores so loud you can't sleep in the same room with her.
She drools. She shakes her head and slobber flies like a rain-
storm. She emits atomic odors...odors that are paralyzing. Yet
despite all of her flaws, we absolutely love this dog! She's part
of the family.

We recently became worried about her when her eyes started
to give her trouble. We took her to the vet, and in order to save
her vision, she was going to need surgery. Part of that involved
plastic surgery to lift her eyelids. Since we didn't want her to

lose her sight, we eventually took her in to have the necessary surgery.

After her operation, she had to wear this large cone around her neck for two weeks so she would not be able to scratch her eyelids. But she also couldn't lick her paws and couldn't sit and scratch behind her ears with her back paw. She would try to go out her doggie door and BAM! She couldn't fit with the cone. She tried to eat but she couldn't reach her food bowl with the cone. We fed her by hand. She walked about dejected, so sad and slumped over. We finally gave her protective device a nickname we picked up from the movie *Up*—the cone of shame.

SHAME ON YOU

A lot of us relate to God out of our own version of the cone of shame. Some think God's primary role in our life is not only to make us feel guilty, but to make us wear the cone of shame. When Roxy came home from her follow-up appointment at the vet, and we took the cone of shame off her after two weeks, she was like a new dog! She ran around so excited, even spastic. She wet herself. Now that she's had her eyes lifted, we say she's the Joan Rivers of bulldogs. I think it's a picture of the liberation God wants to work in our lives when we live in His forgiveness and His grace. He wants to remove the burdens of shame and guilt we carry around that prevent us from enjoying the uninhibited liberty we find only in Him.

So far we've been considering how our connection to God is based not on our good deeds, but exclusively on His grace. The danger is in assuming we have grace all nailed down when studies show most American Christians absolutely don't. Every one of us, no matter how much we think we know in our head, can grow in our experience of God's grace.

We've overviewed some of the barriers and obstacles we face along with Gomer and Hosea. The powerful images the Bible gives concerning what we are rescued *from* and *to* make grace truly amazing. We've considered God's character and love to clear the way in our relationship.

Two obstacles with God we've mentioned but not really explored are those of guilt and shame. Sometimes the cone of shame just seems to fall right into place in our lives. We feel guilt about our mistakes, our anger, and things we've said or words we can't get back. Maybe we came from painful home environments where love was never communicated or where parental blessing was never given. We are confused about where God has been in the pain of our lives.

All this can add up to a deeper identity burden—shame. Where guilt is associated with feeling bad about things we've done, shame is a burden we carry deep in our identity. Guilt says, "What I *did* was wrong; I really messed up." Shame says, "I *am* wrong; I *am* a mess."

Guilt and shame can serve positive purposes in our lives only in driving us to God for His forgiveness, grace, and healing. After all, the Bible teaches that we not only do what's sinful, but have a sinful nature. However, unhealthy guilt and shame drive a wedge between us and God and hinder us from living in His forgiveness and our new identity. They not only drive us away from God, but separate us from the people we love the most and lead us into self-abuse and self-hatred. This kind of distorted guilt and shame plays right into the hands of Satan. His very name, according to the Bible, means "accuser." So the Bible challenges us to "Resist the devil, and he will flee from you. Come close to God, and God will come close to you. Wash your hands, you sinners; purify your hearts, for your loyalty is divided between God and the world. Let there be tears for what you have done....Humble yourselves before the Lord, and he will lift you up in honor" (James 4:7–10). There is great joy on the other side of humbly seeking God's grace and forgiveness.

The barriers of guilt and shame can be obvious and typical, but they can also show up in tricky ways. When you always compare yourself to others or vacillate to emotional extremes of unimportance: *If I can't do this or that as good as so-and-so, then I'm nothing*. When you go to church, but don't take communion because you feel unworthy. When you're always working hard to keep up appearances, taking yourself so seriously that you never laugh anymore. When you pray for others but not yourself; do good to others, but treat yourself harshly. All of these can be indicators of unresolved shame or guilt in your life.

We see Paul wrestling with guilt and shame in Romans. He says, "I want to do what is good, but I don't. I don't want to do what is wrong, but I do it anyway" (7:19). There is guilt over specific actions he's done, but the wrong just keeps flowing out of his life. He tries to get it together, but he keeps failing.

There is also shame. He continues, "Oh, what a miserable person I am! Who will free me from this life that is dominated by sin and death?" (7:24). Guilt and shame weigh him down and threaten to crush him. And both of them are justified based on his life, as they are in our own lives. The solution isn't to just stop feeling this way or to build up our self-esteem and engage in positive self-talk. The answer isn't in trying real hard to bury it in the past. Paul concludes this way: "Thank God! The answer is in Jesus Christ our Lord" (7:25). God through Jesus is the one who can remove shame and guilt and clothe us with our true identity as His people.

This is part of the miracle of grace which is freely given to us, but which cost God everything. He paid dearly to set us free and restore us. He paid with the most precious gift He could give—Jesus. The One who died for us, in our place, and then came back to life fueled by a powerful love that could come only from His Father. He bears our shame and forgives our guilt.

Hosea also knew what it was like to pay the price to redeem the person he loved most. We saw in the third chapter of Hosea that the prophet married to the prostitute had to go and find her once again. Only this time, in order to bring her home, he had to pay her debts in order for her to be released from the sexual slavery in which she had become ensnared.

The level of strength this displays in Hosea can't be underestimated. He would be more than justified in letting Gomer suffer the consequences of her idolatrous, disastrous behavior. In our present world, most of us would be told we're "enablers" if we continued pursuing someone behaving like Gomer. Yet Hosea refused to give up on her, refused to allow her to self-destruct the way she seemed determined to do. He loved her more than she was able to love herself, beyond her guilt and shame.

THE PRICE IS RIGHT

When Hosea goes out to the seedy part of town to get Gomer back, he has to pay to regain her freedom. The picture we see is one of redemption. Used throughout the Bible, "redemption" is an economic word. In the Old Testament, when someone is redeemed, it literally means for someone to pay the price to buy them back, to pay their debts in order to release them from their master or debt holder.

And what was the going rate for a married woman turning tricks in ancient Israel? The price Hosea paid to get Gomer back sounds like the list from some bizarre scavenger hunt: "So I bought her back for fifteen pieces of silver and five bushels of barley and a measure of wine" (Hosea 3:2). This value was roughly equivalent to the price of a slave in the ancient world.[1] If Gomer was ever going to find true freedom, healing, and restoration in her marriage, then she had to be released from the master who possessed her. A price had to be paid to set her free. Throughout the Bible, this marketplace concept is known as redemption.

Since we live in a free country where thankfully slavery has been abolished, we might be tempted to dismiss this term "redemption" as another old-fashioned Biblical word that's irrelevant to us today. While it may sound quaint or even archaic to us, it remains just as relevant in securing our ability to live a new life instead of being chained to our addictions and vices.

Whether we admit it or not, most of us still struggle with exercising the freedom Jesus came to bring us. We still struggle with secret longings, old unhelpful ways of coping, and illicit attachments that provide momentary hits of pleasure. I was reminded of this recently when a woman anonymously posted her secret struggle on our church website, asking for prayer. She wrote:

> I have a secret life as a prostitute. It's a life I left behind many years ago when I first gave my life to Christ and got married.

Now, 20 years later…that old lifestyle called me back. As I sank deeper and deeper into the sexual underground, I began to lose myself again. On the outside I appear normal. I work in an office and am raising children.

How could I let myself go out like this after I had changed my life around before? It's not really about the money; I make enough money on my job to live okay. It fills this hole inside of me, an empty place that can only be filled with being wanted and desired.

I have quit now for a few weeks and cut contact with the people in the lifestyle, but I ask for your prayers for strength and I pray that God will please put some people in my path that will help to lead me back to a lifestyle that I can be proud of living.

Someone going back to prostitution who doesn't have to seems outlandish, but if we replace the words "prostitution" and "sexuality" in her note with our own sin patterns (overeating and comfort food, gambling and adrenal rush, gossiping and feeling superior), we see that she is simply engaging in another form of sin than ours. It promises to "fill the hole" inside us, but it never does.

Shame and guilt work together to keep us in these unhealthy cycles. We feel bad about something we do or about who we are, so we go to church. We listen and maybe feel better, or we pray and promise God we'll never do that thing again if he'll just forgive us. This commitment often lasts anywhere from a half hour to a week, then we do that thing again. Now we feel even worse because we said we were going to stop, but we didn't.

All of it reinforces the idea that we are worthless. We feel like failures so we don't even bother to pray or go to church. Why would God want to hear from us anyway? On and on we go in the downward spiral of guilt and shame.

This cycle would have been real for both Gomer and Hosea. Each in their own way would feel guilt and shame over the family disaster they were living through. Breaking this cycle came with an expense.

RECORD OF CHARGES

Can you imagine what it would have been like for Gomer to have her husband enter this dark world, negotiate with her captors, and buy her back? Consider the emotions—the pain, embarrassment, and humiliation. Was she angry he even came? Perhaps enraged that he would intrude into her chosen life? Was she thankful or relieved? Did she feel like she couldn't accept his love or kindness toward her?

One person describes prostitution as a form of domestic violence. She writes of "the carnage, the scale of it, the dailiness of it, the seeming inevitability of it; the torture, the rapes, the murders, the beatings, the despair, the hollowing out of the personality, the near extinguishment of hope commonly suffered by women in prostitution."[2]

You may not identify with the extremity of what Gomer or someone caught up in the sex trade experiences. But if you are honest with yourself, I believe you will recognize this "hollowing out of your personality" that occurs in different forms of sin. You can get to a place where the only way you can relate to someone else is through that sin. Shame becomes an identity that drives you forward into self-abusive actions.

So when we accept God's gift of redemption, it renovates us on all levels. It pays the price for our guilt and buys us back from our shame. This is why it's essential to understand what actually occurs when we are redeemed.

In the Old Testament, three important aspects to redemption emerge. First, redemption implies a person is in slavery or captive to another master. Second, to redeem a person out of captivity, a price or ransom must be paid. And third, a human liaison must act to secure the redemption.[3]

As we move into the New Testament, the language of redemption saturates. Paul summarizes the major elements in Romans 3:22–26:

> There is no difference, for all have sinned and fall short of the glory of God, and are justified freely by his grace through the redemption that came by Christ Jesus. God presented him as a sacrifice of atonement, through faith in his blood. He did this to demonstrate his justice, because in his forbearance he had left the sins committed beforehand unpunished—he did it to demonstrate his justice at the present time, so as to be just and the one who justifies those who have faith in Jesus.

All the key ingredients of redemption line up here. First, Paul points out that everyone has sinned and is therefore in slavery or bondage to sin. Second, a price had to be paid to free us from the slavery to sin. Third, Jesus is both the price that was paid and the mediator between God and people.

Redemption points to the sufficiency of Christ because it is through faith in "his blood" that our sins are made right. We are not the intermediary; we cannot fix our situation and buy ourselves out of captivity. Imagine someone who's been kidnapped trying to serve as hostage negotiator with their captors. They're overpowered and it doesn't work. Similarly, we are dependent upon Christ's sacrifice and payment.

Paul says that God "canceled the record of the charges against us and took it away by nailing it to the cross" (Colossians 2:14). The phrase "record of charges" was used of a handwritten note that a debtor would write to acknowledge his debt in the ancient world. They would write on papyrus or vellum using special ink (acid-free, we now know) so it could be erased and reused. Jesus erased the record of charges against us, wiping the debt clean. He nailed them to the cross, canceling our guilt and shame.

Jesus "disarmed the spiritual rulers and authorities. He shamed them publicly by his victory over them on the cross" (Colossians 2:15). He robbed evil spiritual powers of their rule by neutralizing them. The language describes what would happen in a victory parade when one country would defeat another in war. After the victory, the victors would return home to parade the win through the city and shame the defeated nation.

Have you ever seen the parade the winning team of the Super Bowl does each year? Or the parade the NBA champion does after winning the championship? They parade their victory publicly and, especially if your team lost, it feels like they are shaming the other team. (Unfortunately, for us Cowboys fans, there has been lots of shame in not even getting to the playoffs!) The cross is where Jesus publicly shamed the powers of evil and declared His superiority. His resurrection became the ultimate victory parade over death and darkness.

Just as Hosea paid a price to redeem Gomer, so also has God paid a price to redeem you. Gomer's price was 30 shekels of silver. God redeemed you with something much more valuable than silver; He redeemed you by the life of Jesus. Often we view ourselves much like the prostitute Gomer: dirty, ashamed, unworthy, and unlovable. Our shame speaks so loudly we can't hear anything else. If we just look at our actions alone, all these things might be true; however, God loves to show His mercy in and through Jesus. He loves nothing more than to give mercy to people who do not deserve it (and none of us truly deserves God's mercy). He paid an outrageous price to cover our guilt and carry our shame. *Outrageous.*

ACCEPTING PAYMENT

At some point, Gomer had to face her fears and square off with the barriers she erected to receiving Hosea's love. She had to dare to let His grace get below the surface of her shame and guilt. But how?

Grace can feel hard to allow into the deep recesses of our broken lives. We often think God can forgive this person or that person, but not me. It took me a while to realize this thinking shows pride in reverse. Basically what you are saying when you say God can't forgive you is, "God, you are going to have to pay a higher price for me."

Apparently Jesus wasn't enough. What a ludicrous statement! If Jesus wasn't enough, then I guess you and God can start working out what the price will be for you. And what in all the universe could cost more to God than giving His son whom He *loved* from the foundations of the world? Who am I to dare tell God this price *wasn't enough for me?*

This is the insane way shame works in our lives. It blinds us to the miracle of the gospel. We feel worthless, but we imply by our hesitancy that the costliest gift given in the universe isn't *worthy* of me. (This is about the time you realize that, as a Christian, you may need some counseling after all!)

Some people say, "I don't need God." This is pride in one way. Other people say, "I'm unworthy and God could never forgive me." That's pride in another way. It looks like humility, but it's actually pride fueled by the pain of unresolved shame and guilt. We have to lay it down and say, "God, you determined the price. You paid the price. The price was higher than what I think I'm worth but I'll receive it with gratitude." That's grace—a humble response to what God has done for us.

Facing our guilt centers on confessing our sin to God and daily applying what He has done for us on the cross to pay for our debt. The Bible says those who are "in Christ" are not under condemnation anymore, so the fight of faith is to believe this, accept it, and live in it.

Shame can be thornier because it gets into our identity. There may be nothing specific to confess; you just feel like you are a loser. Yet Christ bore our shame on the cross as well and God offers to replace our old identity with a new identity. In Chapter 9, we'll explore in detail what this identity consists of and how it can help us live our lives.

We're no longer servants to unhealthy shame and guilt because we've been bought with a price. One of my favorite passages gives us an image of what this looks like: "I am the LORD your God, who brought you out of the land of Egypt so you would no longer be their slaves. I broke the yoke of slavery from your neck *so you can walk with your heads held high*" (Leviticus 26:13).

God freed us so we can walk differently—taking off the cone of shame and walking with confidence in Him. What a simple and stunning image of grace! We don't walk around with the weight of the world on our backs. We aren't moping along feeling insignificant and distraught. We aren't staring at our feet in shame and self-hate. We are not the sum total of what others have said about us.

We used to carry this weight with every step we took, but we've been set free! Our shoulders are back. Our eyes are clear. Our heads are high. ("Clear eyes…full hearts…can't lose!" as *Friday Night Lights* used to put it.) This isn't a proud and cocky strut; it's a redemptive and humble swag because of God's greatness and mercy. It is the spring in our step that results from realizing no matter what others think of us, God is very fond of us!

Walking with your head held high means you stop telling yourself with your inner voice that you are worthless or awful or hated by God. Stop telling yourself you'll never change. Stop walking like someone weighed down by chains, because God broke those chains from your neck. The only shame you continue to carry now is the shame you choose to keep carrying. The door to your cell is unlocked, and you are free to go.

CHAPTER SEVEN

→

award-winning performance

> I do not at all understand the mystery of grace—only that it meets us where we are but does not leave us where it found us.
>
> —*Anne Lamott*

i had a lot on my mind when I noticed that my fuel gauge was on empty. Quickly finding the closest gas station, I pulled in. At this particular station, the "pay at the pump" feature was not working and cardboard signs shouted in sloppy black-markered letters, PAY INSIDE BEFORE YOU PUMP. So I went inside and paid the cashier ten dollars. Then I walked out to my car, got in, and drove off without ever filling up.

I kept running errands until finally pulling into my driveway, I looked down at my gas gauge, now well below E. I felt confused and bewildered for a few seconds before it hit me: I had stopped at the gas station, paid, and never pumped! Can you say distracted and overwhelmed? I was literally driving on fumes.

In many ways this is an illustration for my spiritual journey as well. When I came to faith, I was incredibly thankful for God's grace, but I secretly believed now I had to be really good so I could keep it. I certainly cleaned up my act and refrained from the drugs and parties that had been my escape for so long. And as much as I disliked what I knew about religion, my exposure to Christianity was limited to generalizations and stereotypes.

So I quickly moved into a spiritual service mode, doing my best to perform before God and prove my value. I'd serve the poor, give generously, spend days in prayer and fasting, and generally do a lot of great things for the wrong reasons. I was trying to earn my keep, but my relationship with God began to wither and religion took its place.

On the outside, my life looked pretty grounded and people around me talked about my "spiritual maturity," but I was miserable. I never felt like I measured up or was really accepted by God. No matter how hard I tried, it was never enough. I was only as good as my last performance!

I felt like a fake all the time and started to despise my faith. Christ had paid it all, but that enormous truth didn't seem to apply to my everyday life. I was simply running on empty. I went through the motions of filling my soul's fuel tank, but I rushed off before realizing I was still empty, still driving along based on my own efforts.

JOB PERFORMANCE

I finally came to a place where I just said: "God, I quit! I'm not good enough. I wasn't really a church guy before anyway. I'm a former addict, for goodness' sake. I can't do this Christian thing." How insanely ironic, right? God finally had me right where He wanted me—completely dependent on His grace like when I first came into a connection with Him. He had never asked me to become a super-religious guy. He had only asked me to love Him in return.

We talk about grace, but so much of what happens in churches and what passes as Christianity is wrapped in the message of "God helps those who help themselves." This is nowhere in the Bible, but it is the popular view of how we are to live. Churches champion grace, but with all the talk of serving, getting in a small group, giving, and staying involved, the message of grace gets overshadowed by works. What people hear loud and clear—and see others practice over and over again—is God only wants their best performance.

How many believers have received God's grace for salvation and then turned their life into a big performance trip? How many of us have bought into the American gospel of working hard to be good people and earn our keep? How many of us are running on E even as we leave the place where our tanks should be filled?

I believe Gomer was no different than the rest of us. When she returned home to be with Hosea, the performance temptation would have been huge. The text doesn't say it explicitly, but we're left to imply Hosea and Gomer worked things out, remained married, and began a new life under God. But again that sounds a little too Hollywood; the reality would probably be an exhausting challenge, more like *The Real Housewives of Jerusalem.*

Just imagine the months after Gomer came home again. Yes, Hosea forgave her, paid the price for her, and brought her home. Eventually, she must have accepted this love as a gift. But would she then be able to go on with her life as if nothing so devastating had ever happened between them?

More likely, she spent the following years trying to make up for all the heartache she had caused in the past. What could she do to show her husband she was finally, truly sorry for all the grief she had caused? Would she work harder around the house, strive to be a more perfect wife, or serve more diligently in the community to make up for lost time and lost ground? Would she be motivated for all the wrong reasons?

With this kind of performance mind-set, it would be easy for Gomer to slowly build up resentment toward Hosea. Her efforts would never cover her shame. Perfectionism and performance are often rooted in shame, and if they aren't addressed, they drive us to unhealthy behavior. She had to live with a sense that anything she did would never be enough, as well as a fear Hosea might now reject her because of things she left undone.

The new and improved Gomer couldn't afford to be anything less than completely dedicated, committed, and virtuous. Yet until she fully accepted the gift of grace that had been given to her, she would struggle to forgive herself and move on. Until she became comfortable in her own skin as one fully loved yesterday, today, and tomorrow, she'd keep running on E like so many of us. The pressure would mount and she'd eventually collapse under it.

Hosea may have also been tempted in his own way to put Gomer on the performance treadmill. Maybe he questioned her sincerity in subtle ways. Perhaps he never fully trusted her, constantly looked over his shoulder to ensure she was still there. Maybe he became the ancient equivalent of the wounded spouse who continually checks the voice mails and text messages of their partner, always a little paranoid and suspicious.

After a while this kind of dynamic drives a huge wedge in

any marriage because it points to a trust that is not really being restored, just monitored. Hosea may have felt foolish for continuing to love Gomer after all she had put him through and determined this was the last time. He might have been afraid to hope she would really stay this time.

Hosea could also be tempted to perform to try and overcompensate and blame himself for her unfaithfulness. If he could just be a better husband, the thinking goes, she would never leave him again for her old lovers and her old life. If he could just prove to her how much he really loves her, then she'd never hurt him again.

These relational dynamics are not only real for us as spouses in a marriage; they show up in our journey with God. So how can we break out of this kind of performance mind-set and keep our relationship with Him based in love? I believe the key is to remember our spiritual bankruptcy, our need for the spiritual fuel only God can give. When we realize we are completely and totally empty before God, and all of our performance won't make a bit of difference, we can finally be free.

FILE FOR BANKRUPTCY

In our culture when someone declares bankruptcy, they have different options. There's Chapter 11 bankruptcy, where you reorganize and get things sorted out and you pay back your debts. This form of bankruptcy is only temporary. It provides companies time to work through their issues and move assets around so they can settle accounts and operate with a profit again.

Many of us live as if we have declared Chapter 11 bankruptcy spiritually.[1] We initially realized we couldn't pay our debts back to God and knew we desperately needed help. So we reached out to Him in faith and received His grace freely. We began to heal and grow in our life. But almost as soon as we received this grace, we started to feel like it was time to repay our debts. Sure, they'd been erased by grace, but the weight of them lingers on our backs. So we work hard to reorganize and get back on our feet. This mind-set underestimates the level of sin and junk in our lives that separates us from God. And it leads straight to the performance stage that undermines our life with Him.

A much more serious form of bankruptcy is Chapter 7, permanent bankruptcy. Under this form, a company is broke and beyond the scope of ever working it out. More time won't help. New loans won't help. Its debts are too large and its future feasibility too negative. Under Chapter 7, a company sells off all of its properties and assets to pay off those that it owes, often at a rate of mere pennies on the dollar. Both investors and owners lose all that has been put into the business. Chapter 7 is a total and complete loss.

When we came to God, we all filed under Chapter 7, permanent spiritual bankruptcy. There's no getting ourselves together and relaunching our life using our own power. There's no progressing along with reorganization and trying hard to work it out and please the creditor, in this case God.

We were desperately lost in our sin. We were hopeless, are hopeless, and will be hopeless apart from God's radical grace for all times. We no longer have to repay the debt He's already paid, and we aren't expected to reorganize our life to keep things afloat.

Spiritual economics are really pretty simple. We must stop

living as if we declared Chapter 11 bankruptcy when in reality we all declared Chapter 7 with God! We received grace, God's undeserved kindness, not just for returning to God and beginning the spiritual journey but for growing along the way so we can become all God desires us to be. Grace was all we needed when we first came to Jesus; and grace is still all we need to grow in Jesus.

The same grace that allowed us to begin with God allows us to stay with God. The same grace we stood on when we started with God is the grace we stand on to imitate God. In theological language, grace is for salvation, sanctification, and glorification. It is all of grace. Living in grace and declaring our bankruptcy allow us to rest in God.

OFF THE CLOCK

What does it actually mean to rest in God? In our constantly wired, instantly tweeted world, it's a concept we've lost. Most people have lost sight of what it means to rest, period, let alone rest in God. Even when we're on vacation, we're still checking texts, writing e-mails, and making calls. We're distracted, anxious, and always "on."

The epitome of this was once only New York, the city that never sleeps. But there are those who have lived and worked in both New York and Las Vegas who say this dubious distinction is now shared with Vegas. I would have to agree and even argue that Vegas is the ultimate "timeless" environment. In the casinos, you can't tell time. There are no clocks or windows. The doors to the street are darkened, so sunshine or real life can't enter unimpeded. You can drink at any hour; have breakfast, lunch, or dinner whenever you want; and hit the gaming tables 24/7.

What time is it? Who *cares*?

Outside the casinos, the sun rises and sets, but even on the street it's not much different. Want to wash your car at any hour of the day or night? Go to it. In Vegas, people sometimes clean their cars at 4 a.m. Go grocery shopping at midnight? Workout at 10 p.m.? Drink shots for breakfast? Yep, whatever whenever is the only rule in Vegas. People toil, sleep, eat, and play at all hours. Night blends into day and day into night. Somewhere a husband works nights and his wife works days and the kids go to school, each spouse hardly talking to the other, just eking out a stunted life between the cracks of the family schedules. And this isn't just in Vegas or New York anymore...it's everywhere.

When we live in a performance-based system with God, our spiritual life feels like this. We run hard and the days blur together. On top of the insane schedules with work and family, we have Bible studies or meet with accountability groups. We volunteer and help out. We attend church, keep up appearances, and say the right things, at least on Sunday morning. Don't get me wrong—all of these are great when done out of gratitude in worship to God, but they quickly become oppressive when done as part of a grand scheme to atone for past mistakes and stay in good with God.

One way to avoid this legalistic trap is through rest. The Bible talks about entering God's rest in our present and our future: "So then, there remains a Sabbath rest for the people of God, for whoever has entered God's rest has also rested from his works as God did from his. Let us therefore strive to enter that rest, so that no one may fall by the same sort of disobedience" (Hebrews 4:9–11 ESV).

In the Old Testament, the Sabbath was one day a week when

people rested in obedience to God and in imitation of Him. In the creation account of Genesis, God reserved the seventh day and placed Himself in a position where He was both intimately connected to, and yet infinitely beyond, His creation. He rested. He was, in effect, enthroned. The seventh day in Genesis was God's enthronement day.

In the ancient Near Eastern culture where Genesis was first received, rest was a goal of the mythical gods. For example, the god Marduk achieved rest only after defeating the forces of chaos opposed to him. After his victorious and fatiguing battle, a temple would be built in his honor as a place where he took up residence and rested.

The creation account in Genesis shows God bringing order out of chaos, but there is no battle or grand conflict through which creation arises. This rest is more than just earning a vacation by doing the hard work of bringing the world into a state of order; rather, it is symbolic of His power and sovereign rule, His creative energy. Resting is a display of God's creativity and superiority in creation.

God does not have to contend with forces that oppose Him. He reigns effortlessly. He rests as Sovereign King over what He has ordered. He has established time at this point and initiated creation. No one threatens His rule.

Where God's Sabbath rest is His active rule of everything He has created, our rest is different. We need rest to survive. In fact, every night when we close our eyes, we are either advertently or inadvertently making the claim we aren't God. The fact that human beings must sleep every night indicates we're not the sovereign rulers of the cosmos.

It's important to reflect on this because all too often we act as if we were. But every time our eyelids close, we're putting the lie on it. Every time we eat, every time we drink, every time we rely on outside things for sustenance, we're putting the lie on it. We're God's creations, not the Creator.

REST AREA

This concept extends beyond our bodies to our souls. What was once a Sabbath day of rest is now a state of rest in light of what Jesus accomplished for us on the cross. I still believe strongly in the principle of a day of rest each week, but notice the author of Hebrews calls us to strive to enter this ongoing rest. Ironic, don't you think? It's as if He knew people sometimes have to work at resting! Part of the rest is in the future in heaven, but we can also experience God's rest today.

In God's rest, we don't have to perform. We don't have to struggle. We can simply *be* as His child. Everything we are and everything we'll become is a gift. Notice we don't enter *our* rest, but *God's* rest. We are basing our life on what He has already accomplished. As Jesus said from the cross, "It is finished." We don't need to work to attain God's righteousness; we receive it by faith. This is glorious news no matter how often you've heard it!

Jesus offered us a beautiful invitation to this rest: "Come to me, all of you who are weary and carry heavy burdens, and I will give you rest" (Matthew 11:28). The term "rest" could be translated as "revive" or "restore." He offers to revive us from the inside out.

This rest is for the weary, a word used in reference to people who had been doing hard labor out in the fields all day. They got to the end of the day and they were exhausted. It's also used for travelers who go on a long journey. They walked many miles and were sweaty, dusty, tired, and worn out. Certainly, there's simple physical exhaustion, but many of Jesus' listeners would've wrestled with spiritual exhaustion as well.

Authors Jeff VanVonderen and Dale and Juanita Ryan offer a glimpse into this kind of spiritual fatigue:

> We may try to get it right. We may try to control ourselves and others. We may try to please God and to earn God's love. We do these things because we really do want to have a viable spiritual life; we long to have a relationship with God that works. Unfortunately, most of these attempts to fix ourselves and to somehow earn God's love lead to a spiritual life that is destructive. After a while we find ourselves exhausted and discouraged, and we may feel even more alienated from God in spite of our longing for our relationship with God to be one of the most stable and helpful in our lives.[2]

Rest is offered not only to the weary but to the burdened. The term "burdened" is used in the past tense as if an individual had a heavy burden thrust upon them. Sometimes life just thrusts a burden upon you. Some of you are carrying burdens that are mind-boggling. They feel so heavy and threaten to crush you under their weight. The pain of it is so real with each step you take. Maybe the burden is an illness or a weakness or a temptation. You desperately long for some sense of relief.

It's available because Jesus invites you to find rest in Him. When someone gives you an invitation, there's often an RSVP expected. An RSVP (from the French for *répondez s'il vous plaît*) requires you to respond, to reply if you can make it. The same applies here in a spiritual sense. Jesus is offering us an invitation, and we need to RSVP. We can respond, base our life on His work by faith, and enter His rest—or we can hold out.

Jesus offers to give rest and restore us *personally*. I love how the one translation words it: "Are you tired? Are you worn out? Are you burned out on religion? Come to me. Get away with me and you'll recover your life" (Matthew 11:28 MSG).

LIGHT AND EASY

Exhausted. Discouraged. Alienated. Unstable. Unhelpful. Afraid. Ashamed. Shaky. No, I haven't been spying on you! These are simply the modifiers that describe what our life with God feels like when we base it on our performance. Yet God's rest is here.

This rest is not limited to salvation but all of life. Jesus continues: "Take my yoke upon you. Let me teach you, because I am humble and gentle at heart, and you will find rest for your souls. For my yoke is easy to bear, and the burden I give you is light" (Matthew 11:29–30).

A yoke was a harness they would put on animals. Connected to a cart or a farming tool, an animal would pull with the yoke and carry the load. The master led the animal where it needed to go. If the yoke didn't fit on the animal's neck properly, it would irritate and chafe. He wouldn't get very far with such an uncomfortable burden.

In the ancient world, the yoke became a metaphor for the load we carry as individuals. Jesus is saying if we surrender to Him, follow His teaching, take His yoke which fits perfectly, the work will be easy and light. He'll direct us in the pathways of life.

In the context of Jesus' day, the religious leaders had put so many commands and obstacles on the shoulders of the common people that they just walked around under this incredible sense of burden. They could never be good enough. They could never keep all the laws. They could never jump through all the hoops. They were constantly weighted down.

Jesus offers to take that burden off their, and our, shoulders. He will be our righteousness. He will be our goodness. He will be the one who fills us with peace and joy when everything else disappoints. The end result of this is that "you will find rest for your souls" (Matthew 11:29).

CHILD'S PLAY

So what do we *do* to rest? This is a natural question, but the better question revolves around what God *did* to provide rest, which we considered in the last chapter. Our action is a *response* to God. We place our faith in Jesus and battle unbelief in our lives. This is how we "strive" to enter God's rest.

We trust in God and His word and challenge each other to stay the course. We remind ourselves of God's trustworthiness. We surrender our cares and concerns to God and lay our burdens down. As we do, we experience the truth God shared in Isaiah: "In *repentance* and *rest* is your salvation, in *quietness* and *trust* is your strength" (Isaiah 30:15). Think of the power of these words. It is in turning to God and reflecting on who He is in the quiet, trusting in Him, that we find renewed strength and enter this rest.

I saw what this rest looks like watching Donny, my son's friend, who came over for my eight-year-old son's birthday party. And this wasn't just any birthday party; it was a Pokémon party. My son is enamored with Pokémon and unfortunately I now know way more than I want to about characters such as Pikachu or Turtwig. (Don't ask!)

Toward the end of the party, the kids were having so much fun that Lori and I thought we'd extend it. (I know, crazy us, right?) So we asked Donny if he knew his mom's cell number so we could touch base with her. He didn't. Then we asked him if he knew his home number so we could try her there. He shrugged his shoulders, said he didn't know, and ran off to play. He could have cared less.

At eight years old, all he knew was that his mom would pick him up and get him home as she always did. He knew she'd provide for him, meet his needs, and protect him. That's what moms do. He wasn't concerned about touching base and keeping her up-to-date on what time he should be picked up. That was for grown-ups to worry about.

I smiled at this little guy, and I immediately thought of two things. First, I wondered if my son could recite our phone number! Second, I thought of God. Resting in God means living more like Donny. I don't need to have everything figured out. I don't have to understand all the answers and map out all the contingencies. I don't need to know *how* I'll get home; I just need to know *who* will pick me up.

Resting in God involves knowing He'll show up and pick me up right on time. He'll provide for me and protect me because that's who God is. That's what God does. All I need is childlike faith to trust, let go of my worry, and rest. Or in my case, take the kids to the backyard to swing at the Pokémon piñata I'd hung up and dive for some candy in the grass!

FROM GOOD TO GRACE

In Galatians, Paul speaks to a young church he planted earlier. After they had been established and were doing well, a group of false teachers came in and started to persuade them that, in addition to having faith in Christ, they needed to start living according to religious rules and practices, particularly circumcision.

To Paul, this was not a matter of health code regulations or personal preference; it was a matter of basing one's life on Christ's works or their performance. He goes to great lengths to show that no one was made right with God by observing the law; it was always a gift of God's grace calling forth a response of faith, not a rigid observance of rules and regulations.

Paul gets at this when he writes: "I stopped trying to meet all its requirements—so that I might live for God. My old self has been crucified with Christ. It is no longer I who live, but Christ lives in me. So I live in this earthly body by trusting in the Son of God, who loved me and gave himself for me" (Galatians 2:19–20).

In the gospel, we are given not only an alternative way to live, but also the life of Christ, given to us by God's grace. The gospel is not so much a way of life as it is a life—the life of Christ—given to those who would receive it by faith. Or as Michael Horton has said, "In grace, God gives nothing less than Himself. Grace, then, is not a third thing or substance mediating between God and sinners, but is Jesus Christ in redeeming action."[3]

God's grace is for every day, for the power to obey every command, and for the mercy extended when we don't. It is anchored in what Martyn Lloyd-Jones refers to as God's "disinterested love," which he describes as God's love "unmoved by anything outside itself. It generates its own movement and activity—an utterly disinterested love."[4] God's love is not based on anything lovable in and of ourselves. Grace is given based on the one giving it, not the one receiving it.

Jesus does not minimize the importance or significance of obeying God or His commands; He does not diminish the Old Testament religious law. Instead He affirms and establishes its importance, but now in relation to Him and His work of fulfilling its demands. He doesn't relax the demands of the law, but shows the law for what it is and what it demands in its fullness. He reveals to us that the righteousness that surpasses the religious leaders is given to us by grace. The law was always intended to lead us beyond ourselves to the One who gives us life by grace. It is this grace that keeps us off the performance treadmill and allows us to avoid the danger of legalism.

OPEN THE DOOR

Maybe you've been a Christian for many years, but the passion has just dried up. You are weary and tired. You used to love going to church and got so much out of worship, but it all feels tedious now. Maybe you're carrying heavy burdens and it feels like you're all alone, slogging away.

Jesus is standing at the door today and offering an invitation: "Look! I stand at the door and knock. If you hear my voice and open the door, I will come in…" (Revelation 3:20). This is a favorite passage that many speakers quote when addressing audiences in which people haven't made a profession of faith. What we often miss is that Jesus' words were directed to Christians already. Jesus is speaking to a church, to believers in Laodicea. He's standing at the door of people who have already initially let Him in and He's knocking.

He's inviting Himself over for dinner: "If you hear my voice and open the door, I will come in and we will share a meal together as friends" (Revelation 3:20). Sharing a meal in the ancient world was an act of friendship and solidarity. It was very meaningful, and people were concerned about who they did and didn't have over for dinner. Jesus offers to join us in our lives and fellowship with us as friends. The RSVP is all there if we'll only open the door, not the door to salvation, but the door to ongoing fellowship where His yoke is easy and His burden is light. We open the door to God's rest.

I see this kind of grace-full rest in my friend Judy, who's eighty years old and going strong. She lights up rooms when she enters, an incredible life giver and encourager. She serves at least five days and two nights a week in our Care Ministry and recently made her ten-thousandth personal care phone call to people in our church. (Yeah, you read that right, ten-thousandth.) She volunteers in our Recovery Ministry at church and leads recovery groups in the jails and prisons here in Nevada. She does all this and more, not to perform for God or earn her salvation, but out of gratitude for the gift of grace she has received.

Her journey to entering God's rest was a long one that took over seven decades. By her own admission, she has spent her entire life trying to prove herself to God. For twenty-seven years she served as a nun. She taught Christian school and later worked as a corrections officer. What a combination! And through all that time she says she never really understood the grace of God until a few years ago when she came into our church and heard the simple message of the gospel.

God gave her a gift, the gift of His radical grace in Jesus, and for the first time in her long journey, she entered into His rest. She says she finally has a real, authentic connection with Christ and feels alive. She does so much, but she isn't running on E.

"I can finally rest in the fact that I know I'm not good enough for God, but He is absolutely good enough for me," Judy says. "It is a gift I hope everyone will receive. I just hope it doesn't take you more than seventy-five years to figure it out!"

PART THREE

pursued to become

CHAPTER EIGHT

---

renewing the relationship

> I am not what I ought to be. I am not what I
> want to be. I am not what I hope to be. But
> still, I am not what I used to be. And by the
> grace of God, I am what I am.
>
> —*John Newton*

i confess: i live in fear of my neighborhood homeowners association. I don't know if you have ever received a letter from your homeowners association (HOA) or apartment management company, or if you are in a dorm room situation, your RA. While I had received citations for my trash can being in the wrong place beside my house, one summer I got a notice that read: "Dear Resident: You are in violation of the homeowners policy. The violation is____," and there in the blank someone had scribbled with a black pen, "a yellow patch of grass in your front lawn." The notice then continued, "Please remedy this situation immediately. Failure to comply will result in fines."

Now this did not give me deep satisfaction in the excellent standards that were being maintained in my wonderful neighborhood. I didn't feel like, "Way to go, HOA! I had not noticed that little dead spot in the lawn—thanks for bringing that up. I'm so glad to know that someone is monitoring my yard for me better than I am."

No, my first thoughts involved getting ugly with some hedge clippers! After that, my next thought was "How dare they write me a letter!" I should get in my car and drive around and take pictures of everyone else and all the things that they're doing wrong. What about the lady with the empty house for sale whose entire front yard is dead? Or the people down the street with the knee-high weed garden? Or the family that leaves their Halloween stuff up until Easter? Is that cool with the HOA? Are you writing these people up? All I have is a little piece of yellow grass!

So being the man of the house, I said, "Lori, how could you let this happen? You need to get out there with a lawn hose."

Truthfully, we both knew that in our marriage the yard is my responsibility. I didn't realize the yard had gotten as bad as it had. I didn't plan on it dying. I didn't wake up one morning and say, "Man, I'm going to kill off my grass. This will be cool. No more mowing and maybe I'll get a letter from the HOA!" I was busy with life, and all of a sudden—bam!—I have dead grass.

This occurs in our spiritual lives as well. We're running fast, meeting ourselves coming and going. We don't plan on letting our soul wither or killing the vitality in our experience of God. It just happens because we aren't doing things to keep it thriving. We aren't watering our soul. We wake up one day and realize we're tired, discouraged, and spiritually dry.

We often blame others and think things like "I'm just not being fed," as if spiritual nourishment were something someone else must spoon-feed us. We may think, "My church just isn't deep enough," but is this *really* the problem? Perhaps in some cases it is, but most of us don't obey even a small part of what we already know. Will more depth really make a difference if we don't own the responsibility to live it with God? Sometimes in frustration we just blame the pastor: "If he wasn't so boring or predictable or shallow or arrogant, then I'd be thriving."

What all these things conveniently overlook is that *my* yard is *my* responsibility. The faster I move past blame or apathy and realize I can do some things to grow in God's rest, the better.

As we have surveyed the powerful and unconventional message of the book of Hosea, we've kept an eye beyond their relationship to our own relationship with God. In Part One, we saw why God pursues us—for a meaningful, life-giving relationship. We considered how awe-inspiring God's grace really is in Part Two and how we can live from that grace again. Now let's turn our attention to what it means to grow and thrive with God. We are pursued to become all God created us to be. We can live passionately from the new life and identity He offers.

WAKE-UP CALL

In the third chapter of Hosea, we read that the prophet goes and buys Gomer back from a pimp, paying the same price a slave would sell for in the marketplace. There's no indication Gomer is necessarily grateful and relieved by this. For all Hosea knows, this could be yet another futile attempt on his part before his wife leaves him to go back to the streets. So there are actions that follow his grace-filled purchase.

Hosea tells Gomer, "You must live in my house for many days and stop your prostitution. During this time, you will not have sexual relations with anyone, not even with me" (Hosea 3:3). She is to refrain from sexual contact of any kind, including with her husband. This coming-home season is to be a time of cleansing and healing for both Gomer and Hosea. After the healing period, she will then be restored to full relationship, one that's committed to her husband and honors God.

When a marriage has been rocked by infidelity, restoration obviously isn't instantaneous, short of some miraculous intervention by God. The unfaithful partner must face the consequences of their actions and suffer the impact they have not only on themselves, but on those they love the most. The victims are hurt, angry, and understandably distrustful.

Personal healing and relational repair require willingness from both parties. First, the behavior that betrayed the love must stop. In the case of Gomer, this was sexual sin. She could no longer give herself away to strangers in the search of phony love, temporary affection, or lustful attention. For the marriage to be restored, she had to give up sexual intercourse altogether for a time. Hosea asked her to live in a period of abstinence to restore her body, heart, and soul. This season of abstinence is a sign of her repentance and renewed commitment to her marriage.

God also gives us conditions for us to be fully restored. While we are saved by the free grace of God, such an encounter always results in a changed life. Paul puts forth this issue in the book of Romans. "Well then, should we keep on sinning so that God can show us more and more of his wonderful grace? Of course not! Since we have died to sin, how can we continue to live in it?" (6:1–2). In other words, Christ freed us from our sins by His act of grace, so why would we continue to wallow in our self-centered mess?

God pursues us to help us become the people He created us to be. It's not like He is pursuing us to change us so that then He'll love or accept us. He already does that. He wants us to become our own unique creation in connection with Him. As we discover our uniqueness and grow, we realize we are becoming not only the kind of person God desires, but the kind of person we desire! A person filled with love, joy, peace, patience, kindness, goodness, faithfulness, and self-control.

God wants to rattle us with Hosea and Gomer. As readers, our response should be to consider the journey He's invited us into and ask, "Am I developing and maturing? Am I learning to trust God more and myself less? Am I putting things ahead of God?"

Many of those to whom the book of Hosea was originally written had earlier seasons of faithful living and devotion to God, but they drifted to the place where they were dying spiritually. Hosea is way more than a note from the HOA; it's a loud, no-snooze-button wake-up call from God!

POETIC LICENSE

This process of growing with God is not simply a straight line where a person goes from being bad to better. It's not like Gomer was a prostitute and now she's had a makeover into a new hairstyle and some designer clothes and she rides off together with Hosea happily ever after. This isn't *Cinderella*. This is a story about the grit of real life. There would be the shattered pieces of a relationship to clean up, the rubble of ongoing betrayal. But now on the other side, there could be real joy again.

It's better to see spiritual growth more like a spiral that's gradually moving toward a destination of becoming like Jesus rather than a straight line. You may head this way for a while or you may head the other way, but you're still moving toward the destination, just like a spiral. It's more like a poetic process than a scientific equation.

Grace and truth work together in our development. Without grace we struggle to move past guilt and shame, live in God's wide-open freedom, empathize with the pain of others, experience patience or peace, and accept others and ourselves as we are. We urgently need grace, but not an abridged version that doesn't lead us to face the truth about our lives and our God. Gomer needed grace, yes, but she also needed truth.

If we embrace grace but push back on truth, we'll remain stuck in our old cycles. Truth allows us to be honest with ourselves and others, to possess discernment, call sin "sin," and have meaningful healing. We desperately need truth, and Hosea gives it to us like a right uppercut, but not deprived of grace. Truth without grace will leave us to wallow in guilt and condemnation.

The combination of grace and truth is life giving. We are all wounded in life and sometimes we're tempted to see our wounds as justification for our behavior. Sin and our environment growing up damaged us. Some experienced explicit abuse while others endured subtler forms of neglect. When we are hurting, we tend to be self-focused and self-absorbed, oblivious of the ways our own pain is hurting those around us. We become blinded and distracted by our wounds and often feel like they give us a free pass.

Our culture steps in here and says the solution lies in simply building up our self-esteem. We need to love ourselves more and get back in touch with who we are. The challenge with this is it keeps things in our lives self-focused. The underlying belief is we haven't naturally been making it all about us anyway!

The Biblical perspective is that our self-preoccupation is precisely part of the problem and our wounds have only exaggerated it even more. Hosea and Gomer would both have to confront extreme wounded-ness and betrayal. If they just turned inward to build up their self-esteem and stayed focused on themselves, it would be a recipe for disaster in their marriage.

Living with anyone for any period of time requires us to face our self-centeredness. We can excuse it and justify it, or we can begin to face the truth of God's word, which says our self-centeredness and sin are at the root of the problem. We need the truth of the Bible to challenge our assumptions and address our sin and selfishness.

Of course we need self-esteem, but we also need more, something like *God-esteem*. We look outside ourselves to who God says we are; we trust in the finished work of Christ; we realize that our security and significance come from Him. With these truths in place, we are grounded to look within at our wounds and behaviors more honestly.

NO COMPROMISE

Gomer has gone back to unfaithfulness in her life again and again. Even after she leaves the life of prostitution behind, there will likely be countless compromises along the way. These compromises can show up in deceptive behavior, in lying about things she may not think really matter, in hiding the truth of her sin from herself and refusing to deal with it.

Especially when we come from brokenness, we often rational-ize our compromises by thinking to ourselves, "At least I'm not doing what I used to do." You receive grace and strength from God to overcome one destructive behavior, but getting below the behavior to what's driving that behavioral pattern is a lifelong journey of discovery. There are no shortcuts.

Pride can enter as another compromise. Sometimes the most dangerous and critical people of faith are those who grow in their faith a year or two, experience a certain amount of healing, and then become angry and judgmental toward everyone else. They expect everyone else to get their act together and they forget all the years they were a train wreck!

Maturity involves experiencing grace and truth in one's life, but it also includes living *toward* others with these same charac-teristics. People often excel at being either gracious *or* truthful. The gracious person tends to be accepting, quick to forgive, and ready to reconcile with others. They want to make things right. However, if truth is not in play as well, the grace-only person will be inclined to push "it" under the carpet, leave room to keep it bottled up inside, or pretend like injustice has never happened. Grace-only people will dismiss the problem instead of address-ing it. Practically, this is the person who always makes excuses and refuses responsibility either for themselves or others. Second chances become a crutch.

The truth-only person tends to be ethical and up front when it comes to others. They want to make things right as well. Yet if grace is not in play, the truth-only person will focus on the issue to the extent they view people as problems. Truth-only people will hold ugly grudges, set unrealistic expectations, and often forget their own faults in their witch-hunts. They are often too forceful and inflammatory to fix the problems. Practically, this looks like someone who is impossible to please and hard to get along with. He is dogmatic and has to win every argument; her critical eye will never cut anybody slack.

The goal is to become people of both truth *and* grace. Maybe I've been watching the Food Network too much, but I believe we must season our grace with truth and soak our truth in grace. Then, and only then, will we be able to have healthy and joyful interactions that reflect God's character to a world desperately in need of Him.

So God desires more than just coming to faith and accepting forgiveness. It's also about entering into a process of becoming like Christ. And it is a lifelong process both *for* us and *toward* others.

THE PASSENGER SEAT

Growth really takes off, paradoxically, when we slide over to the passenger seat of our lives. Can you remember how tense it was when you were first learning how to drive? Your mom is in the passenger seat freaking out, "Slow down! Slow down! There's a stop sign!"

"Mom, the stop sign is two blocks away, chill out!"

Those are stressful days for both driver and parent, and in grad school I got a taste of the other side of the car. I lived on a dorm floor with many foreign students. One friend of mine was from a tribe in Africa, and he was trying to get his driver's license. This was a long and tedious process culminating in a driving test for which he needed to prepare so I agreed to help him learn to drive. How hard could it be, right?

We'd putt all over campus at like 1.5 miles an hour. He drove like a little old lady with both hands on the wheel, barely seeing over the steering column. After doing this awhile, we needed to get off the campus and actually try to drive in town if he was to have any hope of getting his license.

So we headed out and he quickly decided he was ready for the highway. I tried to use both grace and truth to persuade him to wait, but he smiled at me and drove straight onto the highway. Now I was like a mom snapping at him to slow down and be careful, now speed up so we don't get run over, and stop gripping the steering wheel so tight. RELAX!

Wouldn't you know we got sandwiched on a three-lane highway with a car in front of us, one behind us, and two eighteen-wheelers on each side of us! I saw my life flash before my eyes! By God's grace we survived and my friend later passed his driving test—much to my own amazement.

It is tough to let someone else drive.

When it comes to spiritual growth, we have a hard time pulling our hands off the wheel and not panicking. Yet growth comes when we surrender, realizing God is driving and trusting Him to get us through the twists and turns.

In one of the most beautiful passages in Hosea, we read: "Come, let us return to the Lord. He has torn us to pieces; now he will heal us. He has injured us; now he will bandage our wounds. In just a short time he will restore us, so that we may live in his presence. Oh, that we might know the Lord! Let us press on to know him. He will respond to us as surely as the arrival of dawn or the coming of rains in early spring" (6:1–3). After a season of disciplining His children, God was still available to the Israelites to return to Him, and He's still available to us today.

The great news is God will heal us, bandage our wounds, restore us, and allow us to live in His presence. He's not finished. He'll draw us to Himself. Restoration is truly a miraculous process that begins in God.

GIFTS THAT KEEP ON GIVING

Many of us have been in relationships that leave scars similar to the wounds that characterize Hosea and Gomer's marriage. Even if our heart of hearts desired reconciliation, the pain of the past is like a huge wall only God can tear down. Only He can command our hearts to "go and love" (Hosea 3:1). In his confessions, Augustine prayed, "My entire hope is exclusively in your very great mercy. Grant what you command, and command what you will."[1]

We see the tension between God pursuing us, restoring us, bandaging our wounds, and our own pursuit of Him when Hosea says, "Let us *press on* to know him" (6:3). There is a mystery to our spiritual formation. On the one hand, God does the work. Even to have the desire to return to God and be restored is evidence God has done prior work in the heart (see John 6:44).

On the other hand, we are called and responsible to cooperate with God, to press on. We simply can't lie in bed all day saying, "God, restore me!" and expect it to happen. We must cultivate our life with God. And the great news is, as Hosea says, that as surely as dawn comes or the spring rains fall, God will respond and restore. He will bring us home.

As part of our process of development, God offers us several important gifts. First, God gives a new heart as He promised:

"And I will give you a new heart, and I will put a new spirit in you. I will take out your stony, stubborn heart and give you a tender, responsive heart. And I will put my Spirit in you so that you will follow my decrees and be careful to obey my regulations" (Ezekiel 36:26–27).

This prophet looked forward to Jesus and the gift of the Holy Spirit we receive through faith. God's spirit comes and takes our "stony, stubborn heart" and gives us a "tender, responsive heart." Our desire to obey comes not from trying harder, but from the way God's spirit revives our desires to want to change. The law provides God's commands but doesn't change our hearts to fulfill them. Like religion, it works from the outside in, but God works from the inside out. We accept the new heart God offers, and as we grow, we find our desires begin to change.

God not only gives us a new heart; He empowers us to obey His commands. Paul writes, "So I say, let the Holy Spirit guide your lives. Then you won't be doing what your sinful nature craves" (Galatians 5:16). We are not weighed down under impossible rules and left on our own to keep them. The Holy Spirit comes alongside us and helps us. We are basically to just stay out of the Spirit's way and let Him lead. We ask for God's strength and guidance. If we sense Him prompting us to talk with someone or help someone or reach out to someone, we step out in faith and do it. When we are convicted of our sin, we take it to God. When we're tempted, we focus on God's power to get us through.

Our new life results from yielding: "letting the Spirit control your mind leads to life and peace" (Romans 8:6). We seek to obey from a position of strength and power as we follow God because we already have received the gift of His righteousness. We already have His rest. We're already secure and loved as we are.

We aren't basing anything on our own merit or strength but on His. The outcome is life and peace.

THE HONEYMOON'S NOT OVER

What have you done in your spiritual life that makes you feel strong, alive, and connected to God?

Ultimately this is *the* question that needs to be answered by each of us to rediscover spiritual growth. It can help us discern our individual road map to maturity. Seeing our life with God as a marriage reveals several practices that allow it to flourish. The initial honeymoon (or second honeymoon in the desert, as you'll recall) may be over, but that doesn't mean the passion dies or the love diminishes. This will look different for everybody, as we are all unique.

I can pursue a variety of spiritual practices—journal, take some time in solitude with God, attend church, pray, study, serve, meditate on the Bible—but frankly, not everything makes me feel strong and connected to God. This doesn't mean I should blow these practices off, but I want to lean more into the practices that really nurture my connection with God.

Leadership guru Marcus Buckingham challenges us to consider our personal strengths and learn how to leverage those strengths in life. He defines a personal strength not simply as something we are good at doing, but as something that makes us *feel strong* and *alive* when we do it. This is a helpful clarifier not only in leadership, but also in our faith.

We can apply our spiritual strengths to important aspects of our growth with God. One is remembering our story. Every marriage has one. For my wife and me, it started when I picked up the phone, took a deep breath, and tried to ignore my moist palms. I had never met her, but I knew her family and I had seen her from a distance. I wanted to ask her out but I wasn't exactly sure what to say. So I exhaled and dialed the number.

Her mom answered, at first a little cold, thinking I was a credit card salesman. When she realized I was not trying to sell her on American Express, she promised to have Lori return my call. Within an hour Lori called and I dropped my pickup line: "Lori, I was just, uh, calling to see, uh, if I could, uh, take you out for coffee to encourage you." It is probably the lamest pickup line ever used, but it worked! Our meeting lasted several hours, and the rest is history.

If we approach Christianity as a relationship, we ask, "What is our story?" You have your own story of how God pursued you and called you into a relationship with Him. You also have the story of God's pursuit of humanity in the Bible. It is the story of God making all of creation, including humans, for the purpose of enjoying what He had made and having a life with Him.

The religion approach to Christianity says, "Read the Bible so that you know what to *do*." The relationship approach says, "Read the Bible so that you know *who* God is." Although the Bible does tell us what to do and that is a good reason to read it, there is so much more to reading the Bible than knowing what to do. Even where the Bible tells us what to do, though, it is telling us who God is—what He values and how He made the world.

Personally, I feel strong and connected to God when I'm regularly reading or studying the Bible or things related to the Bible. This is often a surefire way for me to sense closeness with God. But for others the idea of study drains them of life. They sit down with the Bible and quickly find themselves bored or nodding off. That's okay! You don't have to lean into God's Word the way everybody else does! The important thing is to discover ways you can grow in your knowledge. What were you doing when God's Word really came alive to you?

If you struggle reading the Bible, then listen to the Bible on audio during your run or commute. Dial in to a great teacher online you can tune in to and be inspired by. If you are people oriented, jump into a group Bible study. You may find studying the Bible with others in community fills you with life and strength while doing it alone suffocates you or vice versa.

TALK BACK

Another important area in a marriage is practicing open communication. If a husband and a wife are communicating well, this exchange usually impacts every aspect of their interactions positively. Prayer is our way of communicating with God. Religion sees prayer as a way of asking God for things we need or want. We barter with God by giving Him a certain amount of prayer time, and we expect certain results from that. The relationship approach, though, sees prayer as a way of communicating with a loving Father. Certainly we do ask God for things, but prayer is not our bartering chip, as if we could barter for God's favor. Rather prayer is our way of deepening our journey with God. We pour out our heart and concerns to Him, we thank Him for all that He has done for us, and we praise Him for His greatness.

For years I was challenged by teachers to journal my prayers and write them out. I've probably got five journals I started, but after a few excruciating attempts they'd just collect dust. Eventually, I'd go out and buy a new journal. Surely a new journal would magically inspire me to write my prayers regularly! The bottom line is I hate journaling prayers and felt guilty about this for many years.

But when you think about it, we have no record of any of the great people of the faith in the Bible journaling (just sayin')! How ridiculous is it for people to find something that works for them and then put a guilt trip on everyone else who doesn't do it?

For me, prayer brings life and connection when it is associated with movement. I go for walks and pray while I'm moving. This is the only way I have found to really experience the joy of prayer. If you put me in a prayer circle with other people for an extended period of time, I'm fighting as hard as I can to keep focused and not let my mind wonder. If I'm sitting down or on my knees, I'm only good for a short period of time or I'm daydreaming.

The important thing is not what I do, but what *you* do to remain connected in prayer. Try going for a walk and just thoughtfully praying as you stroll. Read some of the psalms in the Bible and pause every few verses just to echo their prayer and apply it to your life. Try a prayer group at church or praying in a specific space at home. Discover how you can experience more of God through prayer, not to earn His approval or feel better about yourself, but to worship and journey with God.

THEY'RE PLAYING OUR SONG

The night Lori agreed to marry me, we were in a swanky restaurant with a live band. I asked them to play a song that became *our* song, "Unchained Melody," by The Righteous Brothers. It may not be the most original selection, in that countless couples would call this their song as well, but it is *ours* nonetheless. Every time we hear it, we stop and remember or we laugh and do a little slow dancing. (Actually, Lori dances and I stumble on her feet.)

This is just one of many habits we have. All marriages honor certain traditions and rituals. Many couples celebrate their wedding anniversary. Some remember key events—when they went on a first date, moved to a certain town, or bought a home. Couples also develop day-to-day rituals like saying "I love you" in the morning or having breakfast in bed every Saturday. These habits build and strengthen the marriage.

Our life with God works in a similar way. Attending church, gathering with a small group, devotionally making space for the seasons of Christmas and Easter and other important religious seasons can be meaningful in developing a rhythm that facilitates growth. Taking a day off each week to rest and recalibrate personally and spiritually is an important habit. Baptism and communion are more than just empty rituals; they are means of fellowshiping with God and receiving His grace.

You can let go of guilt and stop worrying about trying to act like everyone else. Cultivate your spiritual life by doing things that cause you to feel strong—to feel close and connected to God. If you do this long enough, if you "press on to know him," you'll find you're experiencing grace like water over dry ground. When you focus on knowing and loving God, relating to Him through your story, communication, traditions, and rituals, you'll find yourself growing and thriving.

CHAPTER NINE

⟶

living with a new identity

Our identity rests in God's relentless tenderness for us revealed in Jesus Christ.
—*Brennan Manning*

recently, i received a call from a representative of Ticketmaster asking me, "Mr. Wilhite, are you planning to go to a wrestling event in Seattle?"

"Huh?" I stammered. My only interest in wrestling was as a kid when WWF came on TV after Saturday morning cartoons. I would turn the volume down lower so Mom and Dad couldn't hear, allowing me to watch the headlocks and body slams as long as possible before they'd discover what I was watching and make me change the channel. They considered it too violent for a kid—ah, those were the days!

Anyway, I didn't have to think long to tell my new friend from Ticketmaster I had not purchased those tickets. But someone had, someone who'd assumed my identity, hacked my bankcard, and was headed to the big event.

I was thoroughly spooked! I canceled the bankcard and started looking at every aspect of my identity. I grabbed my wallet to make sure I had my license and social security card. I started thinking about where I kept my bank statements. I wondered, "Where are those old checkbooks anyway?" I thought about how I needed a shredder at home—and a safe!

DO YOU HAVE SOME ID?

We don't have to get a wake-up call from Ticketmaster to have our spiritual identity robbed. Believers struggle every day with remembering who we are and how to live in this new identity. Our spiritual identity is stolen by shame. By thoughts, memories, and voices from the past that tell us we are no good. That no one—including God, *especially* God—could ever love us.

We get it stolen by giving in to temptation. J. I. Packer said, "When a Christian sins he is momentarily suffering from an identity crisis."[1] We are forgetting who we are and whose we are "in Christ." We allow ourselves to be defined by what we do instead of what Christ has done.

We begin to see ourselves through these labels instead of through the truth of the gospel. We have labels for how we look; I'm too tall, short, fat, skinny, ugly. We carry labels for our shame: I'm just a bum or a loser or slut or a lost cause. We're an addict or a drunk or a thief or a liar or a cheater. And we let that hang over us and we carry it around. We not only forget we've been forgiven but fail to embrace the consequences of our new life. We have a partial gospel. We don't live in our inheritance and identity in Christ.

In *Classic Christianity*, Bob George describes how many of us have a limited understanding of our relationship with God:

> Let's imagine that a king made a decree in his land that there would be a blanket pardon extended to all prostitutes. Would that be good news to you if you were a prostitute? Of course it would. No longer would you have to live in hiding, fearing the sheriff. No longer would you have a criminal record; all past offenses are wiped off the books. So the pardon would definitely be good news. But would it be any motivation at all for you to change your lifestyle? No, not a bit.[2]

In the context of Hosea, we see that his forgiveness of Gomer was profound, but it wasn't enough for her to change her life. She kept going back to unworthy things, just like we do in our own ways with God.

So Bob George goes further with the illustration: "Let's say that not only is a blanket pardon extended to all who have practiced prostitution, but the king has asked you, in particular, to become his bride. What happens when a prostitute marries a king? She becomes a queen. *Now* would you have a reason for a change of lifestyle? Absolutely."[3]

Obviously the lifestyle of a queen is much better than that of a prostitute. Any woman who had this opportunity would jump on it. The point George is making is we have more than a half-gospel. We aren't just "forgiven," we are literally the "bride of Christ." God had given us a new identity to go along with the forgiveness of our sins. In Christ, we are a new creation.

GRAPES IN THE DESERT

As we read the book of Hosea, we see powerful images of God's perspective both in the picture of marriage but also in His anger and mercy. After Chapter 3, the drama of Hosea and Gomer's marriage moves to the background and the drama of our relationship with God dominates the story line.

There is blistering judgment from God toward His people. He thunders, threatens, rebukes, confronts, and grieves like one who has been betrayed. On the surface and out of context, these passages could lead one to an impression that God is petty, angry, and bitter. But we've seen there is more here behind these emotions.

God is profoundly serious about His people. His anger results from His holiness and His love. He's offering us everything as part of His magnificent family, and it grieves Him when we reject it.

And between the scorching judgments, we again find beautiful statements of His love. He says, "O Israel, when I first found you, it was like finding fresh grapes in the desert. When I saw your ancestors, it was like seeing the first ripe figs of the season. But then they deserted me for Baal-peor, giving themselves to that shameful idol" (Hosea 9:10).

The image of grapes in the desert leaps out at me. It is a picture of affection, joy, and value in a barren and dead wasteland. Living in the Nevada desert, I've seen its endless landscape where nothing appears to live or grow, but even here God's people are like lush grapes—thriving, wonderful, and refreshing to Him.

As we move into the New Testament, we learn more about

our new identity. Paul writes, "Anyone who belongs to Christ has become a new person. The old life is gone; a new life has begun!" (2 Corinthians 5:16–17). Through faith in Christ, you are not just Jane Smith or John Jones anymore. You are a royal son or daughter of God!

Imagine the profound impact this could have had in Gomer's life. The temptation to see herself as a failure would follow her the rest of her life. She would be hounded by the pull to act according to her old identity. When she failed, she'd want to go back to her old shame and say to herself, "You're just a whore. Things will never change." When she looked to the future, she'd feel the fear of going back, the anxiety of returning to the old captivity. All of this is a part of her history, but it is not who she is as God's child.

The opportunity we have as Christians is to start defining ourselves not by what we have done, but by what Jesus has already done; not by what we do, but by what Jesus does; not by what we are going to do, but by what Jesus will do. The motivation for change isn't only forgiveness, but a life so much better than we ever dared to imagine as we realize what it means to be in Christ.

We say around Central Christian Church, where I serve, "It's okay not to be okay." In other words, we are all broken. We all make mistakes. We sin. But the good news is this: We don't have to stay that way. We can live in the truth of our new identity.

HIDE AND SEEK

The Bible challenges us to let the past go and embrace our real life. Paul writes, "Think about the things of heaven, not the things of earth. For you died to this life, and your *real life is hidden with Christ in God*. And when Christ, who is your life, is revealed to the whole world, you will share in all his glory" (Colossians 3:2–4). Our real life is hidden with Christ in God. When we accepted the invitation to follow Jesus and accept the free gift of His salvation, we, in fact, died to our old life.

The past tense refers to the moment we made Jesus the leader of our lives. The term "hidden" implies the continual effects of this association. The past, which may have been filled with selfishness, betrayal, damaging words spoken and internalized, harmful actions, and broken promises—is dead. The trick is to let go of the familiar and grasp the potential for which we were made.

Don't cling to the past so tightly you can't seize what God has for you today. The future, which is still to be revealed, holds the promise of no more pain, suffering, depression, and fear. This is to be fulfilled when Christ returns and we are "in" Him. The present, with its challenges, struggles, hopes, and dreams is lived "in Christ."

Since we seem to struggle with spiritual amnesia, God's Word is filled with reminders about our new nature and our new way of living. Here are a few aspects the Bible reveals about your new identity to keep in mind the next time you look in the mirror:

You are chosen. Believers give thanks because God has chosen you and loved you even from the foundations of the world. As Peter says, "You are a chosen people" (1 Peter 2:9). God has chosen you and selected you, even though He knew all of your past and future sins. He knows all about your failures, labels, and baggage, and He picked you anyway. His choosing of you isn't to inspire arrogance but humility, for He chose you for His own glory.

You're a saint. Paul addressed his Biblical books "to the saints." He didn't intend for the letters to be read to one or two of the religious elite, but rather was calling all those who followed Christ "saints," even if they were imperfect. Churches in those days were hardly any prettier than they are today.

Some of them were filled with gossip, backbiting, boozing, sexual immorality, and lawsuits among themselves. They argued over inconsequential issues, formed cliques, and left and started new churches. Yet Paul still calls the members of those churches "saints" because that was their *position* before God.

How is he able to do this? The Bible actually presents two realities—an experiential reality and a positional one. *Experientially,* I still fail. I don't always act like a saint. I lose my temper or compromise God's standard. But *positionally,* I'm a saint. I'm forgiven and made right by the grace of God.

You're a priest. In the book of Exodus, we read of the Jewish people being delivered by God. They had been slaves and God set them free. When He called them out, He made a remarkable statement. He declared them a "Kingdom of priests" (Exodus 19:6). "Priest" was a privileged and highly influential position in the culture from which they had just been rescued.

This was almost an unbelievable declaration to a group of former slaves. And the Bible says, we are not just any kind of priest, but "you are royal priests…" (1 Peter 2:9). We are priests as we pray for one another, serve one another, and make an impact together.

When we think of ourselves, we aren't to simply see someone who has failed, made mistakes, or maybe gone through a divorce or been struggling with an illness. We don't see someone who didn't graduate high school or didn't do as well in college or didn't make the basketball team. We are in Christ—chosen, saints, priests, and part of God's royal family. Not only are we loved and forgiven, but we have a legacy that will never perish, spoil, or fade, kept in heaven for us. The more we see ourselves as God sees us, the more we will act the way God desires for us to act.

JUST THE FACTS

One important distinction that helps us understand our new identity and our continual struggle with sin is the difference between indicatives and imperatives. Indicatives explain what is true. They *indicate* the truth of something. Imperatives are commands, things we should or must do.

In the Bible, the indicatives always precede the imperatives. What we must do is always rooted in what is true about us in Christ. For example, Paul writes, "Be kind to one another, tenderhearted, forgiving one another, as God in Christ forgave you" (Ephesians 4:32). The basis for our forgiveness of others is rooted in the fact that God in Christ has forgiven us. The indicative is the truth that we *are* a forgiven people. So the imperative to *be* forgiving toward others should be the logical outworking of that indicative.

The great danger lies in the reversal of these two concepts, or placing the imperatives before the indicatives. Consider an example from parenting. Say a father sees his son hitting his little sister. How should he deal with the son in that situation? If the parent were to follow the Biblical pattern of indicatives and imperatives, he would say to him, "Son, since you are a member of this family, I cannot allow you to continue in this behavior. I love you too much to allow you to persist in hitting your sister. You must stop." This affirms his identity in the family. Since he is (indicative) a member of the family, he must not behave (imperative) in such a destructive manner.

How different it would be to say to the son, "If you want me to love you and allow you to keep being in this family, then you better get your act together and quit hitting your sister!" This approach simply breeds legalism. It communicates to the son the love of the father, and his identity as a son, is contingent upon his right behavior.

When you consider the story of the Bible, God never deals with us this way. The indicatives always precede the imperatives. What I am to do is always rooted in who God says I am. We don't strive to attain our identity. Our obedience flows out of our identity.

Grace comes before law. We see this in the Old Testament as God first freed the Israelites and gave them a new identity and only then does He give the Ten Commandments. This is crucial to understand for all of spiritual formation. Thus, the challenge of the Christian life can be summed up as learning to grow into who God says we already are. As we do, we can fulfill what God says in Hosea: "Plant the good seeds of righteousness, and you will harvest a crop of love. Plow up the hard ground of your hearts, for now is the time to seek the LORD, that he may come and shower righteousness upon you" (10:12).

PRISON OF THE PAST

Can you imagine never hearing the words "I love you" from your mother? Can you imagine the horror that would accompany having to be taught as a child how to put stitches in because your mom brutally beat your dad and stabbed him? Can you imagine it all coming to a horrible end when you're fifteen and your house burned down with your mother? Sheila can. What she has found is that no story is too big or too messy for the grace of God and the new identity He provides.

Sheila grew up in one of those families where you hid your emotions. She never heard her mother say anything nice and this shaped her in a devastating way. The cruelty, lack of emotion, and dysfunction in the home led her to start drinking alcohol at *seven* years old. She drank until she was sick just to mask some of the pain in her young life. By ten, she was addicted to a list of drugs. Faith was nonexistent in her family, and when the family did attend church, Sheila admits she didn't know what it meant. She wondered, "If there is a God, then why would He let me go through all of this?"

During this doubt and self-abuse, Sheila had her first child. She was just twelve years old. The promiscuity, drugs, and destruction she knew as normal continued until she found herself married to a drug abuser, neglecting her children, and in and out of the prison system. For Sheila, prison was often a safer place than her life outside those walls.

One of the times she was in prison, Sheila did something she had hardly ever done as a child, and certainly never done as an adult: she went to church. It was the first time she had been attracted to church or to God at all. She liked the music and how happy and peaceful the ladies in the prison church were. They were actually nice to her. It felt like the first kindness she had ever been offered in her life.

After spending nineteen months in prison, Sheila was paroled and she stayed clean for a little while. But after trying some Bible studies and different religions, it just didn't work. She quickly went back to doing drugs and a damaging life. She hated herself because she had become everything she said she'd left behind. While she may have heard about God's offer of forgiveness, she didn't embrace the new identity He had for her and live from that.

She found herself in jail again, and again she went to church. But this time something was different. This time it was not just the music, but it was because she really wanted what these people had. Some of the Christian women in this community of faith shared the same cell as her, but they were not in the same "prison." She needed what they had and needed to know where they got that joy. When she asked them about it, they always came back to Jesus. Grace. A new life. A new identity. A freedom.

It was there in the prison that Sheila learned how God saw her and it changed how she saw herself. She experienced this strange feeling called "hope." It was a feeling Sheila couldn't ever remember having before.

She was a prisoner to sin outside the prison walls, but inside God pursued her and gave her freedom. God kept putting people in her life that followed Him and had joy. The ladies in the prison church kept telling her that God loves her unconditionally. That was something Sheila had never had in her life. So there in the Florence McClure Women's Correctional Center in Nevada, she surrendered her life to Jesus at one of Central's prison campuses we run in partnership with God Behind Bars.[4] After a life full of pain and void of hope, she finally came home to God.

In prison, God began to shape her life. Her way of thinking, the way she handled myself, the way she talked to people, and the way she treated people were different. The change was not overnight and she'd slip back into old patterns at times. But Sheila was different. She was not lost anymore. She had been given a second chance. She was free to go. She changed from being a person who didn't care about anything into someone who had compassion. She felt love for other people who were hurting. God took away the shame and self-hate, and now Sheila can look in the mirror and like the person she sees.

Today, Sheila is no longer in a physical prison or a spiritual and emotional one. She is learning and growing and helping others do the same. She is able to take her struggles and use her story to give hope and encouragement. When Sheila serves at church, she says, "I feel all the week's stresses just leave me as I am able to help others."

She knows how she felt when she got out of prison and how, with her church friends, she finally feels at home. It is around these real-life people in the real world facing real things that she is able to heal, stay strong, and serve others. She has found a community where people understand her and they, too, need to be understood. And together they are becoming the people God wanted them to be all along. Sheila is discovering what the Bible means when it says we are a new creation and the new life has begun.

The relationship we're invited into with God isn't simply about *not* doing certain things, but living from a new reality. In Hosea and Gomer's case, it wasn't about simply *not* selling herself short anymore. There was so much more healing and renewal that was to come. She would discover who she was in God, her new identity. She would start to see others, especially men, as people for whom there is hope, people God loves. Her whole framework for life, love, and laughter would be affected.

Like Gomer, we must start to see others and ourselves as made in the image of our loving Father. But as we all know, this is often easier said than done. When you think about who you are, what comes to your mind first? Is it your past, your mistakes, and your sin? Do you see one who is forgiven, but then you stop there? Is it a half-gospel? Or maybe you just think of your descriptors (age, gender, race, name, social security number, etc.).

The Bible says you are so much more. You are a chosen person, saint and prized; you are loved and adopted, an heir of all God provides. Spiritual maturity is intimately connected with living from the core of this new identity in Christ. Next time you look in the mirror and are tempted to see the junk of the past, remember who God says you are—His child! Remind yourself that you are someone who has been rescued, set free, liberated, and given the ultimate second chance to live—and love—again.

CHAPTER TEN

the time-out chair

I wish I went with God's plan 15 years ago, instead of mine.

—*Mickey Rourke*

recently my son Ethan came in the house with some unexpected news.

"Uh, Dad, I accidentally threw a rock and broke the glass in the back of the minivan."

At first I didn't believe it—he was just too up front and direct. No excuses, no immediate tears, although he was clearly on the verge, just a little soldier delivering tough news from the front. I just looked at him and then slowly walked to the door and looked into the garage. Sure enough, the back glass on our 2004 gray Honda minivan glimmered back at me in a massive network of silver spiderwebs.

He tentatively followed me outside, where I asked, "How did you 'accidentally' break the glass on the back of the van?"

"Well, I was trying to throw this rock into the garage, between the van and your car, and I kinda missed."

That's an understatement! I just looked at him and started mentally gearing up to give Ethan a lecture on how much this little accident would cost, how he'd have to work for the next ten years to save up his allowance and help pay it off, and how this also earned him at least a year in time-out. Then I looked down and saw he was about to lose it.

"I'm not worthy to be part of this family," he sobbed and opened the floodgates of tears that had been building.

My heart was undone. Forget the stupid back glass on the minivan. My son was hurting so badly that all I could think about was making sure he knew I loved him.

DIVINE DISCIPLINE

By the next day, I was reflecting on how God forgives us again and again and doesn't make us pay the price of what we've broken. In that moment with Ethan, all I could do was take a deep breath, put my arm around him, and tell him I loved him. I talked to him about what an important part of our family he is—how glass can be replaced, but kids can't. I explained to him that while there was a price to pay, he didn't have to pay it. I would do that. All I asked was that he wouldn't throw rocks anymore.

It was like a children's sermon update of the prodigal son story in the Bible for an eight-year-old audience, yet so much of the parallel hinged on Ethan's attitude. If he had been defiant or rebellious, or if he had lied about breaking the glass, I would have approached it differently. Then he'd be grounded or have things taken away for a period of time. I'd discipline him to try to get him to really think about what he had done and determine in his heart to do things differently next time.

This is what parents do. And this is also what God does with His people. He loves us enough to discipline us so we learn and grow. Because He cares so much, He puts us in "time-out" through different circumstances or situations for us to think about our lives and our faith. Sometimes it hurts and sometimes it's outright agonizing, but the end result is a changed life for the better.

Throughout our journey into the story of Hosea and Gomer, we've considered the process of growth as involving grace, truth, and time to heal, and noted the significance of facing the truth in our lives and cultivating our life with God. We've also seen the importance of understanding our identity in Christ and living from that awareness in order to become the person God desires. However, there's one other vital element we must not overlook. God's discipline is a very important and often misunderstood aspect of God's love that fuels our growth.

People don't like to discuss God's discipline because it's not a cozy message. The word itself, "discipline," conjures up our worst imaginings of God as an old, cranky judge out to "get us" for breaking some archaic, esoteric laws. But that's not an accurate picture of the discipline of God. In fact, as we'll see, if God did not discipline us, that would imply He does not love us. Understanding why we face discipline and learning how we can grow from it are of major importance in our spiritual life.

RADICAL LOVE

God's discipline is anchored in the image He demonstrates as a loving father. Throughout Hosea we've seen the Israelites on the run. They have not trusted God to provide for them and have placed their trust in other things. When we get to Chapter 4 of Hosea, the picture of God moves from the metaphor of marriage to one of a father who loves and cares for his kids. While this might strike us as a little creepy, a bit Freudian with all kinds of Oedipal implications, God is simply trying to help us understand His love in the most powerful ways possible.

His love is more than a romantic picture can convey. This kind of love captures a glimpse of the intensity of His passion, but the love of a parent might better express the mercy and forgiveness with which we remain anchored in Him. No matter what my children may do, including breaking minivan windows, I'm going to love them. While I don't and won't always approve of their decisions and actions, I will always love them.

Again and again, God has similarly shown Himself to be faithful, like a devoted father. He's been there all along. He says: "When Israel was a child, I loved him....I myself taught Israel how to walk, leading him along by the hand. But he doesn't know or even care that it was I who took care of him" (Hosea 11:1–3).

Notice how many times God makes it personal: I loved...I taught...I [led]...I took care of the Israelites. God is directly involved. He was always there, even when they didn't acknowledge Him. It is possible that Hosea's life experience is the background for this passage. One of Hosea's children could have been wayward, allowing Hosea to again experience the depths of emotional love that God experiences with His people.[1]

Not only is God pictured as a loving father; we are often depicted as wayward children. God "reared children and brought them up, but they have rebelled against me" (Isaiah 1:2). The emphasis in both Isaiah 1 and in Hosea 11 is on the activity of the father. Hosea takes pains to illuminate God as eager and willing to show unconditional affection to His erring child. Isaiah describes it in this way: "Though your sins are like scarlet, they shall be as white as snow; though they are red as crimson, they shall be like wool" (1:18).

God was literally there when we took our first step, and He was there when we began the spiritual journey in our faith. He leads us "along with my ropes of kindness and love" (Hosea 11:4). This phrase brings up an image of a farmer who has an animal that's harnessed. Rather than whipping this animal to get more work out of it, He's leading it with ropes kindly. He's guiding it tenderly along.

This is how God loves us. He bent down to work with and feed us. But this does not imply that God will not use discipline. It shows His disposition is not one of an abusive father, but a loving one who will do what it takes to help us grow.

TIME OUT

Consider how you were disciplined while growing up. From my experience, I've been through several versions of "time out" in my life. First there was the time-out chair, where I'd be sent for any number of antics. Later came the time-out trip to my bedroom, from which I wasn't to emerge until I was ready to act my age. Then there was my elementary school's version: stand in the corner while everybody else snickered.

Eventually, time-out assumed a different name—detention. There were multiple variations of detention. There was the bored-to-tears detention when I'd have to stay after class and couldn't listen to my headphones or talk or eat or do much of anything but homework. There was the busywork detention where I'd have to do mindless worksheets put in front of me or repetitive writing of the important lesson I was supposed to be learning.

Once my teacher got so frustrated with me, she put me in a room, shut the light off, and left me there! I sat in this dark room for what seemed like forever. When she eventually came back, my parents had arrived. Anytime my parents were involved, I knew it was bad. Whatever punishment I received at school, I got at least that and more at home.

I can only remember my father taking me to the woodshed, so to speak, once, though. My mom had threatened me: "If you keep this behavior up, then just wait until your dad gets home." The old "dad threat," but this time she meant it.

When he got home, he took me out to his woodworking shop in the backyard (I guess it was a literal woodshed, after all). It's the only time I can ever remember him spanking me. Just before, he put his arm around me and told me it would hurt him more than it would hurt me, and then he proceeded to give me three swats. I deserved them and it did look like it hurt him to do it.

But I'm telling you, I believed it hurt me a lot worse in the moment. Irrespective of our view of spanking as a disciplinary punishment, I grew up in a town where this was the accepted practice at the time. (I can remember getting swats several times in elementary and junior high school by school administrators.)

Growing up, I always knew a few things for sure—one of them was that my mom and dad loved me. I knew my dad loved me when I needed to be disciplined, and I knew he loved me no matter how hard things got. It was a constant. I had no problem trusting in him, even when I disagreed with him, because his love was the foundation of that trust.

This gets much more complicated if you had parents who were abusive or if their love was always conditional. Or you never really knew where you stood with them. Some never knew their father or mother, and others wished they didn't because of mental, physical, or sexual abuse. I cannot fathom the pain and betrayal of this nor do I pretend to.

Yet I've pastored long enough to know the experiences we have with our earthly parents often get projected onto God. It can make trusting Him even harder. Please hear me on this: God is not like your parents, even if they were great, and it's worth considering how you may have projected them onto Him. God is someone else—remarkable and magnificent and upright, even in His discipline.

The whole point in discipline in school or discipline from parents to children is to help them change their lives and make better choices. The Bible says, "My child, don't reject the LORD's discipline, and don't be upset when he corrects you. For the LORD corrects those he loves, just as a father corrects a child in whom he delights" (Proverbs 3:11–12). We are to embrace God's discipline because it's proof of His love and is, in fact, motivated by His love.

God uses many things to stir us up to return to Him. It will look different for each person, but there are times when we wait, times when we are brought to our knees, and times when the odds feel overwhelming. God can use these things to direct our attention to Him. After God chronicles all the rebellion of His people in Hosea, He says: "When I please, I will discipline them, and nations shall be gathered against them when they are bound up for their double iniquity" (10:10 ESV). He leverages other nations to conquer Israel and deprive her so she realizes again whom she belongs to.

What do you think is the most loving thing God could do for you? Maybe give you good health? Maybe allow your family to be happy? Some of you may say career advancement or a long life. There is an endless list of things God could do for you to demonstrate His love.

Yet the greatest, most pleasurable, most enjoyable experience of any person is to be able to know God, relate to Him, and make much of Him. There is nothing else that compares with this experience. Nothing even comes close to being able to have a life with the God and Creator of the universe. This is the peak of the mountain of pleasure. This is what we were designed for.

God does the most loving thing He can for us when He disciplines us so we will love and know Him more. John Piper asks, "Do you feel loved by God because you believe He makes much of you, or because you believe He frees you and empowers you to enjoy making much of him? It is the difference between the modern world where all terminates on self, and the Biblical world where all terminates on God."[2] This question is important. If life is all about God making much of me, then God's discipline seems contradictory because it affects my comfort. It is not an easy road. How can He allow me to face these roadblocks and challenges?

However, when I realize His first priority is His glory and I'll be most joyful when I make much of Him, I understand more fully. God's discipline of me is the most wonderful thing He could ever do for me if it leads me to more of Him.

So we should revel in the thought that God's discipline has an end result of deepening our life with Him. The most valuable possession on earth is not money, a home, a career, a golf membership, or even a loving family or anything else other than God. How we respond to God's discipline has everything to do with the health of our relationship.

ACCEPTING DISCIPLINE

The Bible says we aren't to "reject" God's discipline. While there are lots of ways to do this, one of the most common ways is through pushing back. When we are going through a difficult season or we're facing consequences for things we've done, we shove back rather than try to understand what God is teaching us through the effect of our choices. We don't try to learn and grow. We get arrogant and callous toward God. We justify what we've done and become defensive.

This is what the Israelites continued to do in Hosea. God says of His people, "Their arrogance testifies against them, yet they don't return to the Lord their God or even try to find him" (7:10). God will continue to pursue us in our rebellion, but He may also allow situations in our lives that bring us low so we will again look up to Him.

Another way to miss the significance of God's discipline is to just wallow in our problems. Sometimes it is hard to just see beyond our situation. We flounder in the difficulties rather than learn from them. We mope and complain and ask, "Why me?" rather than "Why not me?" or "God, what are you showing me in this?" We shift blame to others instead of taking responsibility. In Hosea, we see the religious leaders trying to shift blame and refuse responsibility. At one point God blasts them and says, "Don't point your finger at someone else and try to pass blame! My complaint, you priests, is with you" (4:4). He's pressing them to take responsibility, turn back to Him, and live differently.

So how do we get the most of God's disciplinary love? How can we "submit" to God's discipline, as the Bible commands?

One important thing we can do is ask God to soften our heart. Hebrews tells us, "As you endure this divine discipline, remember that God is treating you as His own children. Who ever heard of a child who is never disciplined by its father?" (12:7). It isn't any fun. Nobody likes being disciplined!

Yet God is shaping us through it so we become mature people worthy of His honor and glory. We may grieve over it or rage against it or rebel, but we'll never move through it in a healthy way until we soften our heart to God and open ourselves to His purpose. With a soft heart in His hands, He can shape and mold us through the experiences that can prepare us for greater things.

It is important to remember that God's discipline proves we are His sons or daughters. Most of us fear God's discipline, but the more frightening thing is for Him to step back and do nothing. If a parent stops caring what her child does, this is a sign of neglect, not love. Jerome, an ancient Christian theologian and historian, gets at this when He states: "The greatest anger of all is when God is no longer angry with us."[3] Indifference is way more dangerous than anger and discipline.

Hebrews points directly to this: "If God doesn't discipline you as he does all of his children, it means that you are illegitimate and are not really his children at all" (12:8). So as hard and frustrating as the discipline may be, take courage—it proves you are loved and embraced by the Father.

We also can recognize the end result of discipline. God never disciplines us for discipline's sake. He isn't just whipping us into shape for no reason; He prefers to lead us with "ropes of human kindness" as we've seen. He is compassionate and merciful and does not get joy out of discipline. His discipline is "always good for us…afterward there will be a peaceful harvest of right living for those who are trained in this way" (12:10–11).

A peaceful harvest is what God desires for us, which is why He will put us through the paces to return to Him. In Hosea, we read of God's people who had "planted the wind and will harvest the whirlwind" (8:7). Would we rather have our lives resemble a whirlwind or resemble peace? The whirlwind is a picture of God's judgment, but peace is the result of living before Him and becoming the people He desires.

Some are bothered by this picture of God and His love, just as they are disturbed by His anger and judgment. But the alternative is a God who simply lets us do whatever we want and in the end doesn't care. It's like a parent who pays no attention to their child and continues to allow them to do things that will destroy them.

Thank God He cares enough to put us in time-out when we need it. And we can rest in the fact that even when we are being disciplined, God won't quit on us.

NEVER SAY NEVER

This understanding of God's continuous loving presence in our lives is one of the hardest for us to grasp. Maybe it's because we have such a hard time following through with all of our well-intended goals and commitments. Maybe it's because other people are not always there for us in the consistent ways we would want them to be.

I recently dusted off my weight system in the garage and committed to lift weights. I even paid a guy eighty bucks to come fix the pulley system, which had been collecting dust for three years. It worked great…at least it did the one time I used it after getting it fixed! I keep remembering it each time I back out of the garage on my way somewhere and think, "I need to do that."

We start things, but we often don't follow through. Thankfully, God is not like us. This emerges powerfully in Hosea as God says, "Oh, how can I give you up, Israel? How can I let you go?…My heart is torn within me, and my compassion overflows. No, I will not unleash my fierce anger. I will not completely destroy Israel, for I am God and not a mere mortal. I am the Holy One living among you, and I will not come to destroy" (11:8–9).

God threatens and challenges us with powerful imagery and then immediately wonders aloud, "How can I give you up? How can I hand you over?" God doesn't just change His mind on a whim; He's God. He knew this was going to happen. He knew His people were going to desert Him, but He pulls the curtain back on His love for wayward kids. He says, "My compassion is aroused within me." His compassion leads to His discipline for our best interest as well as for our relationship.

We may go through a season in our lives where we do something or experience something that's so difficult we want to give up on God. All the pieces don't fit together and we're ready to walk away. But the great news is even when we are ready to give up on God, God won't give up on us.

In the New Testament, Paul picks up on this idea and says, "I am certain that God, who began the good work within you, will continue His work until it is finally finished on the day when Christ Jesus returns" (Philippians 1:6). Paul is absolutely certain God won't give up on us; he's got great confidence.

This is more than just hope; it is anchored in a belief that salvation is God's work. The term "begin" is literally "to begin in" and is used twice in the New Testament, each time to refer to God's salvation. He began it in you and He's going to see it through until it is "finally finished," which means "fully completed." God is going to complete the work He started in your life when you reached out to Him in faith. Only God can truly complete the work He started.

God is not like us. We conduct experiments, we give things a try, but God carries out a plan. God never does anything halfway or incomplete.

When you doubt and struggle, when you falter, when you fail and fall into sin, when you lose your temper and say things you deeply regret, when you give up on yourself, when you do the same sin for the 337th time, when you quit rejoicing in God, when you fail to love your family, when your friends give up on you, when your family gives up on you, when you fail to see how your life will make a difference, when you feel worse now than when you first came to faith, when you've quit...God won't quit on you. He may discipline you, but He doesn't walk away.

God is so committed to finishing the work He started in us,

Paul can't even think of one thing in the entire world that could separate us from the love of God and His commitment to us. Not one thing! *Nothing*.

HOLD IT TOGETHER

We can rest in the fact God not only won't quit, but He's holding our lives together and making us more like Jesus through it all. The Bible describes Jesus as bigger than anything I can grasp: "Everything was created through him and for him. He existed before anything else, and he holds all creation together" (Colossians 1:17).

This is remarkable stuff. Peter O'Brien says, "Paul's teaching about Christ as the goal of all creation...finds no parallel in the Jewish wisdom literature or in the rest of the extant Jewish materials for that matter."[4] Some translate the word "for" as "toward," which makes the sentence even more dramatic: "All things were created by Him and *toward* Him." Everything began with Him and will end with Him.

Jesus holds it all together. I went nerdy and did some digging on this idea. It seems there is a force holding all things together. Some scientists call it "strong nuclear force."

Take an atom as an example. Okay, most of us don't remember much from science class, but stay with me, it will be worth it. Some people say opposites attract in dating, right? It's the same in science. If something has a positive charge, it is attracted to something with a negative charge.

But the odd thing is the middle of an atom (its nucleus) is made up of a bunch of protons along with some neutrons. This is a recipe for disaster because the protons all have a positive charge and should repel one another, kind of like putting a bunch of lawyers together in one room. Instead of repelling one another, though, they stay together because of a "mysterious" energy being supplied from outside the atom.

Crazy, huh? If this energy to help the protons stay together was not supplied from an outside source, most atoms would become one explosion after another. This "mysterious" force that holds an atom together is very strong and not something to be messed with. If something disrupts this, like nuclear fission, an atomic bomb is created. When an atomic nucleus looses this mysterious force for just a second and splits, it emits several hundred million volts of energy. So when the Bible says Jesus holds all things together, this is like a…big, serious, superpowerful, heavy-duty force!

The one who holds it all together is holding you and your problems. If He holds the atom together, He can hold you and your family. If He holds the stars in place, He can hold you in your depression. If He holds the moon in orbit, he can hold you in your financial struggle. If He holds the water in the oceans, He can hold you in your marriage troubles. If He holds the sun, He can hold you in the death of a family member.

Maybe you feel like you're in the time-out chair of life right now. The challenges could be mounting and the pressure is undeniable. Remember you're there because of divine love. He'll discipline you and may even bring you to your knees, but He won't abandon you. He loves you more than the most passionate lover.

He loves you like a perfect father.

———————▶

CHAPTER ELEVEN

saint maybes

The tendency to turn human judgments into divine commands makes religion one of the most dangerous forces in the world.

—*Georgia Harkness*

a friend of mine in Nashville e-mailed me the following question, not without humor: "I was just followed on Twitter by a strip club in Vegas, and I was completely lost as to why. Then I realized that you are following them, and I am following you. Is this a Vegas thing?"

I recounted how a while back some people started to follow me on Twitter who initially appeared to be part of a porn spam group. Their bio sections on their profile were explicit, and their profile pictures and language were racy. After looking at some of their updates, I realized they had all recently attended our church.

I asked my wife, "Should I follow them back?" She said, "How do you think Jesus would respond?" Well, we honestly didn't even have to think about that one. After all, Jesus was the guy known as a friend of prostitutes and tax collectors. So I followed them back. In Twitterspeak, this just means we receive each other's status updates.

A couple months later, I met with some people who had gone through a family tragedy. I talked to a daughter in the family and several of her girlfriends and we prayed together. They relayed to me how God was changing their lives and how being part of the church community was impacting them. They shared how the friendships they built were the best thing that had happened in their lives in a long time. They talked of growing up in tough environments, never knowing their fathers, facing abusive family situations—you name it. They were all in their early twenties, tatted head to toe, but filled with a growing joy from knowing Christ.

I left the meeting so encouraged. Sometimes you work and pray and labor and wonder if it is making any difference, but not that day. Christ was real to them. The joy and love growing in their lives just inspired and reminded me why I love what I do as a pastor.

It wasn't until later in the day after the meeting that I realized these were the girls I had followed on Twitter, the ones I'd initially thought were porn spam. As they became a part of the community of faith and began to grow, God worked through other people to bring significant change. When all of this hit me, I felt thankful I followed them on Twitter. I could have missed the impact of what God was doing in their lives.

You never know who people are behind their social media persona or where they have come from. You see some racy pictures, but don't know the story of growing up without a dad, looking for love in all the wrong places, starving for affection and attention, and willing to go to great lengths to try to get it.

As I explained all this to my friend in Nashville, I wrote, "This is why I follow everybody back on Twitter now, even strip clubs, because you never know. But I wouldn't suggest it for everyone!" Those girls are experiencing life change in the context of community, and I'm very honored to play a small part in that. It all began when they started hanging around with people of faith on Twitter and then in person. Amazing!

Changing your life means changing your community. Literally. The impact of other people cannot be overestimated. Honestly sharing with others in the context of both life and faith is essential to becoming the person God desires.

We've covered a lot of ground emphasizing the personal, relational aspect of faith. We've looked at how God pursues us to grow into the new creation we become when we follow Jesus. We've seen the importance of our new identity in Christ and of submitting to God's discipline. There is a necessary personal dimension to all of this that's critical. However, God also calls us to more than a personal relationship with Jesus; He calls us to a *shared* relationship with Jesus.

SAVE ME FROM CHRISTIANS

The challenge with a shared relationship with Jesus is, of course, the people we're called to share it with. Novelist Anne Rice, who wrote about the vampire Le Stat in *Interview with a Vampire* as well as numerous other best-sellers, made headlines when she renounced her atheism and returned to the Catholicism of her childhood. She hit the headlines again when she officially quit Christianity after ten years.

Yet the interesting thing is that Rice is not giving up on Jesus. She said: "For those who care, and I understand if you don't: Today I quit being a Christian. I'm out. I remain committed to Christ as always but not to being 'Christian' or to being part of Christianity. It's simply impossible for me to 'belong' to this quarrelsome, hostile, disputatious, and deservedly infamous group. For ten…years, I've tried. I've failed. I'm an outsider. My conscience will allow nothing else." The following day she went on to say, "In the name of…Christ, I quit Christianity and being Christian."[1]

I sympathize with Anne Rice. Christians can be incredibly loving and joyful and encouraging, but they can also be astoundingly judgmental, divisive, and opinionated. I've seen Christians exhibit some of the most remarkably selfless acts motivated by God and His love and I've watched them do ghastly things. This is the human predicament. So is the answer to quit organized religion and just pursue an individual thing with God?

The difficulty is you can't really separate Christ from His followers because God loves them both. When the Bible talks about good news, it isn't just individual salvation, but salvation of the world, of all who believe and receive God's promise. And while we do that individually, we also do that together.

The marriage metaphor is explored in depth in the book of Hosea, as we've seen, but remember this metaphor is more than an individual one—it's a corporate one between God and His people. The New Testament extends the metaphor to the church as the "bride of Christ."

This concept of the church as the bride of God reveals both the essential beauty of the church and the steadfast faithfulness of Jesus the groom. While instructing men to love their wives,

Paul made the marital analogy of Christ and the church: "Husbands, love your wives, just as Christ loved the church and gave himself up for her to make her holy, cleansing her by the washing with water through the word, and to present her to himself as a radiant church, without stain or wrinkle or any other blemish, but holy and blameless" (Ephesians 5:25–27).

Christ loved His bride, the church, so much He gave His life for her. As a groom preparing for the wedding day, He presents His new bride dressed in white and without any blemish. Jesus cares for His bride and does whatever it takes to protect her life.

What would happen if you attended a wedding and insulted the bride? What if you bided your time in the reception line, only to finally approach the bride and groom and tell the new husband you very much admire him but you think his wife is less than attractive? What do you think the groom would do? He'd probably have to explain to the rental place how he got your blood on his cummerbund.

Many people say they love Jesus but think the church is ugly and not for them. I hear people say sometimes, "I just wish I had God's care for those who are far from Him" or "I just wish I had God's concern for the poor." Those are great desires. But I've never heard anybody say they wished they had God's love for the church. He passionately loves the church as a bride!

People sometimes ask, "Can you be a Christian without attending church?" The truth is, yes, you can be a Christian and never go to church, just like you can be married and never go home to be with your spouse. But in both cases, as someone said, your relationship with your significant other will suffer.

CRUSADES AND WITCH-HUNTS

One of the main reasons people often resist the Christian church emerges from the pages of history, and how the church has led and or responded to events with violence rather than compassion. In fact, I recently talked to someone who refused to be part of the church because he said the church was the cause of slavery, witch-hunts, and the Crusades. I couldn't argue with him that there are some not-so-pleasant skeletons in the closet of Christianity. Many Christ-followers as well as nonbelievers find ourselves having a difficult time loving the church and Christians in the church—and not unjustifiably.

Yet the reality is we all still fail to live up to how we are called to live by God. We don't love the poor enough, we don't care for the sick enough, and we don't share the good news with those who are waiting to hear it. All this led me to want to quit the church in college.

At one point I met with a mentor and told him I was planning to transfer to a different college and switch my major from Biblical studies to business because I could not see myself working as a pastor in the future. The church was just too messed up. He said something that really shook me: "If you leave the church, you forfeit the right to criticize the church. Only from the inside can you effect change." He convinced me over several months to stay in the church and work to bring positive change.

I also realized some of our perceptions of Christianity simply aren't accurate. We learn in history class that over a span of three centuries, thousands of people lost their lives in witch-hunts. The church definitely had a role to play in them and committed serious mistakes. Yet what we don't learn in history is most of the time it was also Christians who were trying to suppress the killings and reduce the cruelty of the secular courts.

David Bentley Hart notes that historically it was secular tribunals, not religious institutions, that carried out the bulk of the European witch-hunts. He writes, "Ultimately, in lands where the authority of the church and its inquisitions were strong—especially during the high times of witch-hunting—convictions were extremely rare. In Spain, for example, in the whole of the fourteenth and fifteenth centuries, we have evidence of only two prosecutions going to trial."[2] Were there some horrible miscarriages of justice? Of course, but there were also many Christians fighting against injustice and working for peace.

Some see Christianity as inherently responsible for racism and slavery, and yet it was Christian activists who sacrificed enormous amounts of time and energy to overthrow slavery. Historian Rodney Stark writes, "Although it has been fashionable to deny it, anti-slavery doctrines began to appear in Christian theology soon after the decline of Rome and were accompanied by the eventual disappearance of slavery in all but the fringes of Christian Europe. When Europeans subsequently instituted slavery in the New World, they did so over strenuous papal opposition, a fact that was conveniently 'lost' from history until recently. Finally, the abolition of New World slavery was initiated and achieved by Christian activists."[3]

We should be cautious about lumping everyone into the category of Christian oppressor when so many Christians risked their lives for the oppressed—and still do.

Some say religion is the cause of all the wars in the world. In the West, much of this blame gets laid on Christianity's doorstep. Yet the communist cultures of Russia, Cambodia, and China killed millions of their own people without any framework of God. Without God in the picture, things turned even more violent.

We're taught to see the Crusades as a violent movement of Christian soldiers on a peaceful and loving Islamic community. But this simply isn't historically accurate. Islam had colonized and taken over large areas of the world aggressively by war. I'm not saying the Crusades were right, but in the culture of the time, these Christians felt provoked not unlike Americans after the attacks of 9/11. It is easy to judge history from centuries away, but in the milieu of the time, both Christians and Muslims and the nonreligious share responsibility. And throughout history many Christians have given their lives to promote peace, as have many Muslims.

Ultimately, much of the bloodshed and violence done in the name of Jesus is not consistent with His teachings. However, one could argue that Hitler was consistent with Nietzsche's framework of atheism and the will to power as he instituted the horror of World War 2.

I'm not trying to erase all the mistakes made by Christians, and there are too many to recount, but we should recall the good as well as the bad. Christians have been foundational in overthrowing much evil in the world and in starting universities, hospitals, and charities that have served millions of people throughout history. The solution for a believer is not to discount the church and walk away, and forfeit the right to criticize or correct her. The solution is to step into community with the church and benefit you, the church, and the world.

THE POWER OF COMMUNITY

God created us to be connected to each other because of what it does for us spiritually, relationally, and emotionally. After mountains of sociological research and tons of self-help studies, happiness is still best predicted by our relationships. It all comes back to community. God knew this from the beginning; He created us this way. In the context of community we are to bring our confession, to bring words that ask for forgiveness, and to be willing to share this with each other.

The final chapter of Hosea begins with a collective call to people of faith to come home to God: "Return, O Israel, to the LORD your God, for your sins have brought you down. Bring your confessions, and return to the LORD. Say to him, 'Forgive all our sins and graciously receive us, so that we may offer you our praises'" (14:1–2).

The call to return is not one of isolated Western individualism. It is a call to return to the community of faith. In New Testament terms, it is a call to return to the "bride of Christ." Everything in this verse is collective—"our sins," "receive us," "our praises." In other words, our individual faith isn't a solo thing.

For myself, I know I need the accountability of others. I need the community to share in so that I can find the healing that comes from confessing my sins. I'm not just a pastor of a community of faith; I'm a product of the community of faith. As I confess my sins to others and to God, it releases the hold of sin in my life and helps me grow.

God's people are instructed to take words of repentance and confession with them instead of sacrifices. Throughout Hosea, Israel is guilty of faking true worship. She has brought her sacrifices and gone through the motions, but her heart was far from God.

In the context of confession and faith, real life change can happen. A couple years ago we had an outside organization come to the church where I serve and survey hundreds of people, enough that with a slight margin of error they could project out some clear themes from our overall church community. They came back with the results and said that 98 percent of the people used the language "the church saved my life." That is the power of the gospel. It was God and His grace, using the hands and feet of His people, which saved their lives. But it only happens when we get real with confession and experience the power of community.

COURAGE TO ENCOURAGE

Just as we can point to many events and issues, both major and minor, for which we blame the church, we must also recognize how communities of Jesus followers save lives. When I consider this, I'm reminded of a novel by Anne Tyler from the early 1990s entitled *Saint Maybe*. It's the story of a family that has some hard things happen and what it means to rise to the occasion and love each other in the midst of such trials. This strikes me as a good way to define what the church should be, a family filled with Saint Maybes.

Personally, I've had so many seasons where the encouragement of friends is a huge part of what helped me pull through. I remember going through significant church leadership challenges several years ago. It felt like emotional bullets were flying everywhere.

I sat in my office so frustrated and worn out when I noticed I had a voice mail. I was afraid to listen to it for a moment, fearing I'd get an earful, but when I hit play, it was the words of a friend: "Jud, stay the course, don't falter, we are with you and God is still in control. Trust Him and walk in faith. Be courageous!" By the time the voice mail was over, it was just like someone had reached through the phone and lifted me up at one of my lowest points. It didn't make everything okay and there was still quite a battle to fight, but that encouragement became defining for me and that afternoon is one I will not forget as it became a turning point in my resolve. That's the power of a friend's encouragement!

In Hosea we read, "Assyria cannot save us, nor can our warhorses. Never again will we say to the idols we have made, 'You are our gods.' No, in you alone do the orphans find mercy" (14:3). We see a mutual encouragement to refuse idols, put God first, trust in His power to save, and find mercy as God's children. This is the kind of mutual challenge we're to share with each other regularly.

STAY COOL

The reality is we are so much stronger, so much more vibrant and alive, together than as isolated individuals. We need each other. Alone we might survive but together we can *thrive*.

Living in such an arid, desert environment, I'm reminded that getting lost by oneself can be deadly. And it's especially brutal in the summer. Last summer I was driving along a major highway when I heard this huge explosion. I immediately ducked because it sounded like a gunshot. There was warm liquid everywhere. Completely confused as my heart drummed a thousand miles an hour, I pulled over by the side of the road. I thought for a moment I'd been shot or at least shot at.

The fizz sound was the first thing that gave it away. It had gotten so hot inside my car sitting outside in the summer, that when I turned a corner, a Coke can exploded in the backseat! Now, that's hot!

Since it's the high desert, unfortunately there aren't a lot of trees around to park under, so your car just sits out there baking in triple-digit heat. Perhaps that is why I love the image God introduces in Hosea when He says, "I will heal you of your faithlessness; my love will know no bounds, for my anger will be gone forever....My people will again *live under my shade*" (14:4, 7).

The Bible was written for a group of people who lived in a dry, hot, arid climate. They knew the value of shade. God is saying that when His people return to Him and ask for forgiveness and make a break from the destructive elements of their past, He'll be their shade, their covering, and their protection. He'll shield them from the harsh elements and give refreshment.

This refreshment is available to us in community. One friend of mine used to engage in self-injury as a way of dealing with her pain. Her arm is permanently marked with scars that she often hides by wearing long-sleeve shirts. She came to faith and grew in the context of community, and now she glows when she smiles. She asked me what she should say when her young daughter gets old enough to inquire about the markings she carefully hides from others.

I said, "You should look her in the eye and say, 'These scars mean your mom survived. I did some things I regret, but I'm alive because of God's grace and these scars remind me how far I have come.'" Embrace your scars, no matter how painful they are. They tell the story of your survival. And share what putting God first has meant in your life. It will pour courage into those around you.

LESS IS MORE

I truly believe it's impossible to fulfill many of the commands of the Bible outside of community. We're called to love others, serve others, care for others—how do you do that outside of community? And there's no size limit. God makes it clear where two or more people are gathered in His name that He's present with them.

The church I serve started with twenty-four people in a rented space called "Odd Fellows Hall"—seriously, how great is that? They would go in early and clean all the empty beer cans from the party that had happened there the night before and then would set up chairs and have services. They didn't even have a pastor then, but they did have a clear, tangible love for God and for others.

Ed Welch clarifies why we need each other: "Regarding other people, our problem is that we need them (for ourselves) more than we love them (for the glory of God). The task God sets for us is to need them less and love them more. Instead of looking for ways to manipulate others, we will ask God what our duty is toward them. This perspective does not come naturally to any of us, and many of us need to look at this truth from several angles before we can see it. But the…truth is another of

Scripture's divine paradoxes—the path of service is the road to freedom."[4]

In order to be emotionally healthy, we should learn to "need them less for ourselves and love them more." Only if we have our identity firmly rooted in the good news of Jesus will we be able to be freed from the treadmill of seeking people's constant approval and the emotional unhealthiness that this brings. We'll be able to share with others in the remarkable gift of God's love, and we'll experience meaning in shared purpose.

ANIMATION MOTIVATION

One of the most important truths I learned about the church comes from an unlikely source. You see, a long time ago, before the Disney Channel, Nickelodeon, and Cartoon Network, there were…Saturday morning cartoons! I would get up early, grab the Froot Loops cereal box, and sit for hours on our living room floor inches from the television. I remember watching *The Smurfs, Richie Rich,* and *Schoolhouse Rock!*—"conjunction junction what's your function, hooking up words and phrases and clauses."

My favorites included *Scooby-Doo!.* Fred was supercool (he wore an ascot, for Pete's sake!) and always came up with traps for the bad guys, but I loved Shaggy. Somehow Shaggy and Scooby would go off the logical path of deductive detective work but would always catch the bad guys (*"Farmer Johnson!"*) in the end (*"You meddlin' kids!"*).

Another favorite was *Mr. T.* How could you not absolutely love a cartoon with Mr. T as a globe-trotting gymnastics coach who solved mysteries and always taught an important moral lesson? I pity the fool who never saw it! I also loved *Teenage Mutant Ninja Turtles*. Heroes in a half shell—Turtle Power! They were Leonardo, Michelangelo, Rafael, Donatello—and their ninja-teaching-rat-sensei Splinter. Those guys were awesome!

Now forgive me for going all pastoral on you, but what made many of these shows great was that they were all living for a purpose greater than themselves. Scooby and the gang and Mr. T were trying to solve mysteries to help people and *Teenage Mutant Ninja Turtles* were trying to save the world from destruction by Shredder. Even *Schoolhouse Rock!*'s purpose was to teach you correct English grammar, math, and history.

As people, we were created to live beyond ourselves, to have a greater purpose. This purpose isn't simply to be forgiven and wait for heaven. Our new identity brings renewed mission into our lives. We get to join God in His mission to renew all things.

The first challenge to this is making life not about me. As a follower of Jesus, I've had seasons where I've gradually begun to make life all about me again. I protected things I had—my time, my money, my stuff. I grew increasingly concerned with what others thought of me. I was bothered if I didn't get the respect I thought I deserved. Conversations involved me talking a lot about (who else?) me.

It happened almost imperceptibly. Eventually little things added up in a more noticeable way. And inevitably the more I made it about me, the more miserable I became. It is like a gravitational pull in life. The faster I realized what was happening and surrendered my life and my rights to God, the faster I reconnected to greater purpose and was freed to experience more joy, peace, and security in the context of community.

Like me, some of you have been followers of Jesus for many

years and you've crept into complacency and self-centeredness. You find yourself trying to protect what you have. You start to wrestle with significance and purpose and the feelings that result from making it all about you.

Get fired up about living beyond yourself again! Serve a greater purpose than your life, your work, and your career. In doing so, you'll find a whole different level of significance in your life. Embrace a shared relationship with Christ and the church, and you'll rediscover the shared mission of redemption and restoration.

SPIRITUAL SWEEPSTAKES

We've looked at living from our new identity in Christ, and it is no coincidence that just after Paul says we are new creations, he talks about how our identity shapes our purpose. He says: "So we are Christ's ambassadors; God is making His appeal through us. We speak for Christ when we plead, Come back to God! For God made Christ, who never sinned, to be the offering for our sin, so that we could be made right with God through Christ" (2 Corinthians 5:20–21).

One radical thing about this verse is that we are all ambassadors for Christ whether we like it or not, whether we think we have the right skills or not. If we are "in Christ," we are Christ's ambassadors. The word Paul uses in the expression "we are ambassadors" means essentially "to be older or the eldest," but came to be used in connection with functions for which the wisdom of the age was required. In the political sphere, it was used of an ambassador who represented his nation. Our ambassadorship is to appeal to the world to come home and experience this life with God.

God did not simply redeem Israel for Israel; He redeemed them for His glory and so they would be a light to the surrounding nations. He redeemed Hosea and Gomer so they would bring Him glory and point others to Him through their lives. And what a story they had! That Hosea would love Gomer through the mess; that they would be reconciled and find the power in God to move forward. That redemption can happen not only for them, but for everyone. When we make room for God and let Him change our lives, we will naturally become one of God's ambassadors. Because we have experienced God's love, we will want to tell everyone about it.

Think about the privilege we have in being an ambassador for God. A lot of people think that Christians are like the IRS. What does the IRS tell you? "This is how much you owe. This is how much your debt is." It's pretty bleak. While it is true we have a debt to pay, it is also true that Jesus paid that debt. We are more than the IRS—we have good news to share!

I'm convinced that being a Christian is like working for Publishers Clearing House. You know, the people that show up at your door and say, "You won one hundred million dollars!" We're not even like the average messenger for Publishers Clearing House because we've won the sweepstakes as well ourselves. We both won the sweepstakes because of what Jesus did! We are no longer enemies of God. We can be forgiven in a right relationship with Him. We don't have to worry about our future. He'll be with us even through the darkest night and the toughest situation.

We are ambassadors for this redemption and restoration. The

Biblical story doesn't only move from creation to the fall of humanity in sin to the redemption of God's people. There is also restoration. We can partner with God as part of His church community to bring renewal to our cities. Every act of kindness, of goodness, of love, every moment teaching a child or encouraging someone else, every prayer, every time you make food for a friend in crisis, or give your best at your job, all of it matters if you do it unto God.

God wants to make all things new *in us* and then He wants to work *through us* to make all things new in our communities! God doesn't just want to save and forgive us, but He also wants to use us to bring hope and restoration to the world through the community of faith.

Looking in from the outside, it is easy to criticize the church community. It's like living in a house with a room that's a complete disaster. There are clothes on the floor; there are stains, crumbs, and leftover food on the carpet; there are holes in the drywall; and the patches that remain are covered with crayon drawings. The stench radiating from the room is nearly unbearable, and every day you walk past the room and complain it's a wreck.

The same is true with the church and Christians. You may be terribly upset with the failures of the church, but if you fail to be part of the community and do anything about it, are you really better than those you are criticizing? The call is to jump in and relate to God as a member of the community He loves as a bride.

Life's better when it's shared, especially our life with God.

the joy of being caught

> The grace of God means something like:
> Here is your life. You might never have been,
> but you are because the party wouldn't have
> been complete without you.
>
> —*Frederich Beuchner*

when my wife, Lori, was about six months pregnant with our first child, I committed a dreadful miscalculation in judgment. Lori is a beautiful woman who is naturally thin. Our first child was growing within her, and Lori literally glowed. Naturally, she was also self-conscious about gaining weight and showing so I constantly reminded her how beautiful she was.

One day she came in and sat down on the couch. We immediately heard a loud tearing sound and looked at each other curiously. Then she stood up and revealed she had ripped a huge hole in the back of her khaki capri pants.

Now when your wife is pregnant and she blows out her pants, there are several ways you can react. I started laughing uncontrollably. I thought it was hilarious. I slapped my leg saying, "That's hysterical! You blew your pants out!" She had her hands to her face and her shoulders moved like a person laughing. We were all one big comical family—isn't pregnancy fun?

Then in the recesses of my mind a little bell rang that warned me something wasn't right. Lori wasn't laughing at all, but she was cracking up in a different way. Her shoulders played the part, but those were not tears of joy coming down her face. She was crying. She was hurt.

I immediately shifted into, "Lori, I'm sorry, you're not fat, I mean, you're pregnant, you're beautiful, uh, it's the pants they just…uh…" But it was too late. The tears just kept coming and everything I said to make it better made it worse. The pent-up emotions and physiological changes she experienced collided with my stupidity over a waterfall of tears.

She cried so hard she threw up. And she threw up so hard she broke some blood vessels across her face.

This was not my shining moment, especially when her mom came over, took one look at her, and asked, "What's wrong with your face?" I desperately wanted to crawl under the sofa cushions.

Unfortunately for Lori, this was not my first or last dumb-guy move. There would be plenty more. Like when she came in after getting a new haircut and asked, "Do you like my hair?" I paused and said, "Well, I love you." *Geez,* can a guy get a clue here?

I could go on, but I'll spare you. She's stayed with me not because I'm smooth and not because I have a clue. I obviously don't. She's stayed with me because we are *committed* to each other. She loves me—even when I'm stupid or hurt her feelings. We're married. We work through it all. We're in this thing to-gether.

POP THE QUESTIONS

This ongoing commitment is part of what God communicates to us about our journey with Him through the metaphor of marriage. His love holds it all together even when we don't have a clue. He's completely committed no matter what dumb things we do.

The last verse of Hosea challenges us to reflect on all of this: "Let those who are wise understand these things. Let those with discernment listen carefully. The paths of the LORD are true and right, and righteous people live by walking in them. But in those paths sinners stumble and fall" (14:9).

This isn't a melodramatic love story to be left buried in history. It's more than a historical account of a nation's unfaithfulness to her God. This is our story, and we're to listen carefully and discern how it applies to our lives. Only God can satisfy us and fulfill us. Gomer learned it on the streets, on the run, as so many of us have. We stumble around in the darkness and trip and fall. We long to go home, but aren't sure we'll be welcome.

We can embrace the love of God, or we can keep running inside or outside the church. We can be honest about our own doubts, fears, and mistakes and bring them to God, or we can keep making excuses. We can rest in Him or keep striving in our own power.

Here are some things worth reflecting on in light of our excursion through Hosea:

Do you really know the personality of God? Have you neutralized Him to an empty shell of who He reveals Himself to be? The God of Hosea is mysterious and glorious and completely beyond. He is ridiculous in His love and severe with His jealousy. He is anything but *neutral*. His primary concern is not social change, politics, the next presidential election, or environmental care, though these are all important. His greatest desire is that your heart is completely His.

What are you allowing to creep into first place in you life? God wants nothing less than first place in your life, and He jealously guards this rightful place. He's not on some ego trip but knows that placing Him first is what you were created to do. Have you allowed self-centeredness to take priority to the point where you relate to God only when it's convenient for you? Is there sin in your life you're unconcerned or dishonest about?

Have you made an idol of bad religion? When it comes to religious practices, God reveals Himself to be more concerned about your relationship with Him than your sacrifices. Are you motivated by gratitude and worship, or are you trying to prove yourself to God? Are you spiritually exhausted?

When was the last time you just enjoyed God and His love? Have you somehow assumed so much familiarity with grace that it's become *boring*? Have you domesticated grace to the point where you think you totally fathom it? Does God's grace still inspire you to joy, thankfulness, and a yearning to follow? Is it amazing?

Are you living in His rest as one secure? Are you claiming your new identity and battling unbelief? Are you facing life without the reassurance and challenge of other believers?

The point of Hosea, and the point of these questions, is to get us to stop and reflect. Consider the miraculous opportunity we have! God has revealed Himself as one who actually wants to relate to us. He's shown through this story of the prophet's pursuit of the prostitute that He'll overcome any barrier to patiently bring us home to be with Him. He's exposed His fierce love and made Himself vulnerable to our response. He's put all His cards on the table. He's all in.

PULLING OVER

Every time I see a patrol car on the side of the freeway, I get this fear in the pit of my stomach. I lift my foot from the gas pedal and check the speedometer. I mentally make sure I have my seat belt on and turn the music down. I immediately scope the cars around me to see if somebody is going faster than me. If they are, I'm feeling good. I watch my rearview mirror really closely after I pass him.

If I get pulled over, and I have several times, I usually respond the same way. Some of us argue. Some of us get emotional and tear up (my wife does this). Me, I'm just the most naive, clueless person on the planet. I say things like, "Really, I was going that fast? Wow! I just had no idea. The speed limit is forty? How could this have happened? Do you know I'm a pastor?"

That pastor thing rarely works, nor does my cluelessness, but that's beside the point. God's pulling us over for joy, both His and ours! He's pulling us over to make much of Him, to experience this outrageous adventure of faith, and invite us on the ride of our lives.

He's pulling us over to propose.

Has there ever been a greater picture of this marital love in history than Hosea and Gomer? Could there be a more power-ful display of love than Hosea staying with Gomer and caring for their children even though they had different fathers? Has there ever been a more profound image of God's divine obsession with people than Hosea going to the shady part of town and buying his wife back from sexual slavery? What could be more illogical than this? What could illustrate more commitment?

I can only think of one thing—the cross of Jesus Christ. God sending His very son to buy us back. All our pain, rebellion, and running crashing into God's passionate pursuit on beams of wood. God taking the punishment we deserve upon Himself, bearing our guilt and shame in Jesus and inviting us into His freedom.

Both of these displays blow up our human understanding of love. Both of them are scandalous. Both show He is more than curious or halfhearted about us. Both show you are invaluable to Him. You are God's divine obsession.

His love is crazy and irrational. He's not asking you to fully understand it; He's asking you to receive it and live in it. He's calling you to say yes to His proposal, to renew the vows, to live in His joy forever.

If you put this book down and think it was a nice study of Hosea by some crazy guy in Vegas and move on to the next thing on your to-do list, then I've failed. At the very least, I hope exploring Hosea together in these pages has provided you with an opportunity to consider where you are and where God is. To see how much He loves you. To discover the life-giving relationship He offers you, be moved by grace again, and be challenged to live from your true identity.

Today you choose a path. Do you relate to God as a traffic cop who just wants to bust you or as a jealous lover pursuing you to give you freedom and life? Your choice will affect the rest of your life and determine how you are remembered both in this life and the next. You can pull over again and experience the joy of being pursued…and being caught.

acknowledgments

This book began as an idea over seven years ago and took a long path to completion. It was a struggle of quick starts and long stops until, remarkably, it all fell into place and flowed onto the pages in a flood. To everyone who encouraged me to keep pressing on, a simple thank-you doesn't seem like enough.

I'm particularly grateful to:

Esther Fedorkevich: Your passion and enthusiasm literally got this book off the ground again, and your unwavering support and motivation found it a home and kept it moving.

Rolf Zettersten, Jana Burson, Shanon Stowe, Harry Helm, and the entire team at Hachette/FaithWords: Your willingness to trust in me and this message made this process a labor of love, and I'm truly thrilled to be partnered with you.

Mike Bodine, Eugena Kelting, Michael Murphy, Justin Jackson, Kayla Gilmore, Paul Mudd, and the Central family: I'm so thankful to be able to work and live alongside you to point people to God.

Dudley Delffs: Your insight and perspective truly gave this book new life.

Lysa TerKeurst: Your brilliant coaching helped refine this message and give it much-needed clarity.

Mike Foster: Your friendship has impacted my life and this book in profound ways; here's to more deck time.

The Wilhite and Williams extended families: You've always been my strongest cheerleaders, and I hope this book represents not only my own heart, but so many of yours as well.

Emma and Ethan: You simply make life a blast! I cherish you and pray that you increasingly celebrate the God described in these pages.

Lori: Your companionship brings me so much daily joy, and every year I know you, I love you more completely. Thanks for serving the One who pursues so faithfully alongside me.

notes

ONE. THE PROPOSAL

1 Unless otherwise noted, all Scripture quotations are from the *New Living Translation*.
2 For example, Ezekiel 23, Jeremiah 3:6, and Isaiah 50:1.
3 See Ephesians 5:22–33 and Revelation 19:6–8.

TWO. PASSIONATE PURSUIT

1 James Limburg, *Hosea-Micah* (Atlanta, GA: John Knox, 1988), 9.
2 John Piper, *The Pleasures of God: Meditations on God's Delight in Being God* (Portland, OR: Multnomah, 1991), 194.
3 J. I. Packer, *Knowing God Through the Year* (Downers Grove, IL: InterVarsity Press, 2004), 221.

THREE. AN AFFAIR TO REMEMBER

1 Arthur Miller, *Timebends* (New York: Harper and Row), 1987, 482.
2 Greg Beale, *We Become What We Worship: A Biblical Theology of Idolatry* (Downers Grove, IL: IVP Academic, 2008), 12.
3 Ibid., 16.
4 Merriam-Webster Dictionary, accessed online: http://www.merriam-webster.com/dictionary/fanatic (February 25, 2010).
5 David Powlison, "Idols of the Heart and Vanity Fair," *The Journal of Biblical Counseling* (Vol. 13, No. 2, Winter 1995), 49.

FOUR. BAD ROMANCE

1 See Christian Smith with Melinda Lundquist Denton, *Soul Searching: The Religious and Spiritual Lives of American Teenagers* (New York: Oxford University Press, 2006), 162–71, as quoted in Michael Horton, *Christless Christianity* (Grand Rapids, MI: Baker, 2009), 41.
2 Smith, as quoted in Horton, *Christless Christianity*, 42.

FIVE. LOVED FROM DEATH TO LIFE

1 Francine Rivers, *Redeeming Love* (Colorado Springs, CO: Multnomah, 2009), 139–40.

SIX. PRICE FOR A PROSTITUTE

1 James Limburg, *Hosea-Micah* (Atlanta: John Knox, 1988), 14.
2 Margaret A. Baldwin, "Split at the Root: Prostitution and Feminist Discourses of Law Reform," *Yale Journal of Law and Feminism* (Vol. 5, 1992), 47.

3 L. Ryken et al., *Dictionary of Biblical Imagery*, electronic ed. (Downers Grove, IL: InterVarsity, 2000).

SEVEN. AWARD-WINNING PERFORMANCE

1 I'm indebted to Jerry Bridges for the analogy *Transforming Grace: Confidently Living in God's Unfailing Love* (Colorado Springs, CO: NavPress, 2008), 13.
2 Jeff VanVonderen, Dale Ryan, and Juanita Ryan, *Soul Repair: Rebuilding Your Spiritual Life* (Downers Grove, IL: InterVarsity Press, 2008), 11–12.
3 Michael Horton, *The Christian Faith* (Grand Rapids, MI: Zondervan, 2011), 267–68.
4 Martyn Lloyd-Jones, *Studies in the Sermon on the Mount* (Grand Rapids, MI: Eerdmans, 1976), 268.

EIGHT. RENEWING THE RELATIONSHIP

1 Augustine, *The Confessions*, Book X, 40.

NINE. LIVING WITH A NEW IDENTITY

1 J. I. Packer, *Knowing God Through the Year* (Downers Grove, IL: InterVarsity Press, 2004), 221.
2 Bob George, *Classic Christianity: Life's Too Short to Miss the Real Thing* (Eugene, OR: Harvest House Publishers, 1989), 71–72.
3 Ibid., 72.
4 For more information on God Behind Bars, see www.godbehindbars.com.